TABLE OF CONTENTS

*Shown In Photographs On Designated Page

iii

*Shown In Photographs On Designated Page

iv

*Shown In Photographs On Designated Page

*Shown In Photographs On Designated Page

*Shown In Photographs On Designated Page

vii

*Shown In Photographs On Designated Page

INTRODUCTION

The major theme in this handbook is FUN! HOLIDAY presents art and craft ideas for the sole purpose of adding to student's sheer enjoyment of major holidays throughout the school year.

Materials are simple, directions are complete and concise and the finished products are ones that the students can display with pride.

Holidays are a time for fun . . . a happy change of pace in the normal routine. We present these art and craft ideas in that happy holiday spirit of joy.

SECTION I:
"HALLOWEEN"

Projects in this section include a variety of Halloween masks, costumes and enough jack-o-lanterns, witches, ghosts and assorted goblins to transform your classroom into a veritable spook house!

TOP ROW: Tissue Ghost, Pumpkin Head Ghost, Egg Carton Witch
CENTER ROW: Paper Plate Pumpkin, Paper Plate Black Cat
BOTTOM ROW: Simple Spooks (3 examples)

1. TISSUE GHOST (Shown on page 3, upper left)

A. Materials: For each ghost provide half a sheet of black construction paper, a white facial tissue, a small scrap of white construction paper and paste. The ghost's eyes and mouth may be colored with black crayon, felt pen or tempera paint.

B. Procedure: Spread the white facial tissue flat on your desk. Pick it up by the center and paste this tip to the sheet of black construction paper. The tissue forms the ghost's robe. Arrange the folds of the robe as desired.

Cut a 2½" circle from white construction paper. Draw on black eyes and a mouth. Paste this circle onto the top of the robe to form the ghost's head.

2. PUMPKIN HEAD GHOST (Shown on page 3, top center)

A. Materials: Use the same materials as described in "Tissue Ghost" above, except use a small scrap of orange construction paper instead of the white construction paper listed.

B. Procedure: Paste a white facial tissue onto black construction paper as described in Tissue Ghost above.

Cut a 2½ inch circle of orange construction paper. Color a jack-o-lantern face on the pumpkin using crayons, tempera paint, felt pen or pieces cut from colored paper and pasted in place.

Paste the pumpkin head onto the tissue body of the ghost.

3. EGG CARTON WITCH (Shown on page 3, upper right)

A. Materials: Provide pressed paper egg cartons, scissors, tempera paints, brushes and decorative materials such as colored construction paper, yarn, etc. Decorative pieces may be fastened to the basic form with tape, glue or staples.

B. Procedure: Cut a four-cup section from the egg carton. The top two sections of the carton will be the witch's eyes. Paint round, black eyes in the bottom of these two cups.

The raised, center portion of the carton becomes the witch's nose, and the lower two sections will be her mouth. Paint a scowling mouth in these two lower sections.

Scraggly yarn hair may be taped or stapled to the top of the carton, and a black construction paper hat added as a final touch.

4. PAPER PLATE JACK-O-LANTERN (Shown on page 3, left center)

A. Materials: Students will need pressed-paper plates (paint will not adhere to plastic coated plates), scissors, pencil, orange and black tempera paint, brushes, green construction paper, a stapler and string or yarn.

B. Procedure: Two paper plates are needed for each jack-o-lantern. Use a pencil to draw a jack-o-lantern face on each plate. Make a totally different face on each plate, for example one scary, one silly. Use scissors to cut out the eyes, nose, ears, etc., on each plate, following the penciled guidelines.

Paint the inside (eating surface) of each plate black. Paint the outside (back surface) of each plate orange. Allow the paint to dry thoroughly.

Cut a pumpkin stem shape from green construction paper and tape or staple it to the inside top rim of one plate. Put the two plates black sides together and staple around the rim to hold them firmly together. Punch a hole at the top of the plates and thread through a hanging string.

These three-dimensional jack-o-lanterns are especially nice when hung in a window, for they are equally attractive when viewed from either side of the glass.

5. PAPER PLATE BLACK CAT (Shown on page 3, center right)

A. Materials: For each black cat provide two pressed paper plates (paint will not adhere to plastic coated plates), black tempera paints and brushes, black construction paper, scissors, tape, stapler and string or yarn. Facial features may be painted with tempera paint or cut from colored paper and pasted in place.

B. Procedure: Draw a cat's eyes, nose and mouth in the center section of one paper plate. Cut out these facial features, then paint the back (convex) side of each plate black. Allow the paint to dry thoroughly.

Cut two cat ear shapes from black construction paper. Tape or staple them in proper position along the inside (eating surface) rim of one plate.

Put the two plates together, painted sides out. Staple around the rims to hold the two plates together. Use tempera paint or pieces cut from colored paper to add such decorative features as whiskers, teeth, eye pupils, etc. Punch a small hole in the top center of the plates and tie on a hanging string.

6. SIMPLE SPOOKS (Shown on page 3, bottom)

A. Materials: Construction paper, a paper cutter, scissors and black thread are needed for this activity. Additional decorations may be colored with crayons or felt pens, or made from scraps of yarn, colored paper, fabric, etc., and pasted onto the basic form.

B. Procedure: Cut a 4″ x 9″ rectangle of white, orange or black construction paper. A paper cutter makes quick work of cutting 9″ x 12″ paper crosswise into three 9″ x 4″ parts. Cut several sheets at once to speed the work even more.

Cut away shaded areas as shown in figure 1 below to form the spook's head and eyes. Add any desired decorative features such as scraggly yarn hair, facial features colored with crayons or cut from colored paper and pasted in place, etc., as shown in figure 2.

Punch a tiny hole near the center top of the spook's head and tie on a black thread. Tie this thread onto a black thread stretched across the room as shown in figure 3. The black thread will be almost invisible, making the spooks appear to be floating in air.

Example:

figure 1   **figure 2**   **figure 3**

7. FLYING BATS

A. Materials: Black construction paper, pencil, scissors, rubber bands and black thread are needed for this activity.

B. Procedure: Use half a sheet of black construction paper for each bat. Fold the paper in half crosswise and draw a half-bat shape along the fold as shown in figure 1. Punch a hole through the wings as shown. Cut out the bat shape.

Cut a 3″ length of rubber band. Run the rubber band between the two holes as shown in figure 2. Tie a knot in each end of the rubber band to hold it in place.

Tie a black thread to the rubber band and hang the bat from this string. Any breeze in the room will cause the bat to "fly".

Example:

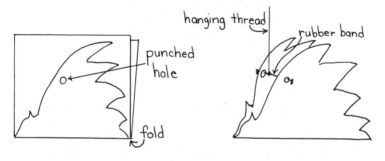

figure 1   figure 2

8. BALLOON SILLIES

A. Materials: Provide balloons of almost any shape and size, scissors, colored construction paper, glue, yarn, fabric scraps, cotton batting, etc., as needed for decorations.

B. Procedure: Cut a strip of construction paper about 2 inches high. Roll this to form a cylinder and paste or staple the ends together. This cylinder becomes a "collar" on which the balloon head will rest.

Inflate a balloon. Decorate it to resemble a silly face using pieces of paper, fabric, yarn and cotton batting. Glue them to the balloon to make facial features and hair.

Set the completed balloon face in the paper collar for display.

9. SPOOKY SILHOUETTES (Shown on page 11)

A. Materials: Students will need newsprint (or any other absorbant paper), water colors, black tempera paint and paintbrushes.

B. Procedure: First prepare the background for the picture. Using a very wet brush, paint the entire sheet of newsprint with stripes, blotches or any haphazard areas of color. While the paint is still wet, tip and tilt the paper to allow the paint to run slightly together. One area of color now fades gradually into the next, producing a shadow effect. Allow this background color to dry thoroughly. (If this portion of work is done just before recess or lunch period, the paper will be dry by the time the students return to the classroom.)

Paint a spooky Halloween scene with black tempera paint on this colored background. The effect is eerie indeed!

Spooky Silhouettes and Hosts of Ghosts

10. HOSTS OF GHOSTS (Shown on page 11)

A. Materials: Provide white muslin (old sheets, cut into pieces work fine), needles and thread, old newspapers, scissors, twigs from dead branches of trees and paint or felt pens for adding facial features to the ghosts.

B. Procedure: Wad a piece of newspaper around the top spike of a twig. Place a square of white cloth over this paper wad and tie it firmly around the twig. This forms the ghost's head as shown in figure 1.

Gather a rectangle of white cloth along the top border and tie this to the ghost's neck to make his robe. (see figure 2) A triangle of cloth tied around the head becomes the ghost's scarf as shown in figure 3.

Facial features may be painted on with tempera paint or drawn with a black felt tipped pen.

To have the ghost stand erect, insert the base of the twig in a small paper cup filled with

figure 1

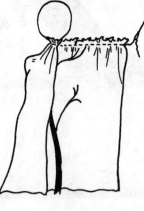

figure 2

figure 3

pebbles or wet sand and arrange his robe to cover the cup. Or, the ghosts may be hung from fine, black thread to "fly" around the classroom.

11. CARTON CREATIONS

A. Materials: Almost any kind of carton (a cereal box, cottage cheese carton, tin can, cardboard tube from a paper towel roll, etc.) can be used as the base for these creations. Cartons can be covered with brown wrapping paper (use pieces cut from grocery sacks), colored construction paper or fabric. Decorations may be painted with tempera paint, drawn with crayon or felt pen, or cut from colored paper or fabric and pasted in place.

B. Procedure: Cover the container with brown wrapping paper, colored construction paper or fabric. Then let the shape of the container serve as inspiration for the form to be constructed.

For example, a tall, slender cardboard tube could be decorated to look like a totem pole stack of black bats. Paint the bat's bodies on the tube, then cut wing shapes from black construction paper and tape them to the back of the tube.

A pint cottage cheese carton could be covered with chartreuse paper, then decorated with tempera paint, yarn and cut paper to look like a scraggly witch. A cereal box, wrapped in brown paper, could become a scar-faced pirate with a cut paper eye patch and a real bandana scarf around his head.

The only limits are those of each child's imagination as he turns these simple materials into Halloween theme creations.

12. SHOE BOX OWL

A. Materials: Provide shoe boxes (or any other boxes of similar shape), scissors, tagboard, masking tape, tempera paints and brushes.

B. Procedure: Cut away large, round eye shapes from either the lid or bottom surface of the box. Cut a V-shaped slot for the owl's beak and bend it up to stand out from the box. Cut ear and wing shapes from tagboard and tape them into place on the top and sides of the box. Use paints to paint the owl as desired.

These owls are especially effective if you set a flashlight inside the box so the light shines through the box openings when displayed.

Example:

13. SHOE BOX BLACK CAT

A. Materials: A shoe box (or any other box of similar shape), scissors, tagboard, masking tape, tempera paints and brushes are needed for this activity.

B. Procedure: Cut away eye, nose and mouth shapes from either the lid or bottom surface of the box. Cut ear shapes from tagboard and paste them in place. Cut narrow strips of tagboard for whiskers and tape them in place (wire or pipestem cleaners could be used for whiskers if desired).

Use tempera paints to paint the entire box black. When this paint has dried, added decorative features may be painted with contrasting colors if desired.

These black cats are especially effective if you set a flashlight inside the box so the light shines through the box openings when displayed.

UPPER LEFT: Trick or Treat Bag
UPPER RIGHT: Sock Witch Puppet
CENTER LEFT: 3-D Tissue Ghost
BOTTOM LEFT: Squeeze Bottle Spooks (3 examples)
BOTTOM RIGHT: Paper Sculpture Pumpkin

14. TRICK OR TREAT BAG (Shown on page 16, upper left)

A. Materials: Students will need small paper bags (lunch size), pencils, scissors and tape or a stapler. Decorations may be drawn with crayons or felt tipped pens, painted with tempera paints, or cut from colored paper and pasted in place.

B. Procedure: Cut a paper bag as shown by the dotted lines in figure 1. Overlap the handle ends and tape or staple them firmly together.

Use crayons, felt pens, tempera paint or pieces cut from colored paper to decorate the bag in a Halloween theme as shown in figure 2.

Example:

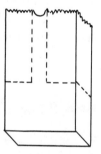

figure 1   figure 2

15. 3-D TISSUE GHOST (Shown on page 16, left center)

A. Materials: For each ghost provide two white facial tissues, white yarn or string, a stick about 6″ long and a small paper cup filled with crumpled newspaper, pebbles or sand. Facial features may be painted with black tempera paint or felt tipped pen, or may be cut from colored construction paper and pasted in place.

B. Procedure: Open one facial tissue and lay it flat on a table top. Crumple the second tissue to form a loose wad and put this wad in the center of the flat tissue. Set a stick upright in the center of the crumpled tissue wad (see figure 1).

Bring the flat tissue up around the wadded tissue and tie it firmly around the stick (see figure 2).

Paint facial features on the ghost, or cut these features from colored paper and paste them in place. The free end of the stick can be plunged into a small paper cup filled with crumpled paper, pebbles or sand to anchor it. Spread the ghost's robe to cover the cup (see figure 3).

Example:

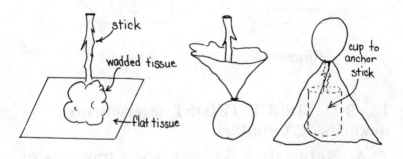

figure 1   figure 2   figure 3

16. SOCK WITCH PUPPET (Shown on page 16, upper right)

A. Materials: For each puppet provide a black, ankle length sock, an 8 to 10 inch sturdy stick, old newspapers, black string and black yarn. Facial features may be embroidered, cut from colored construction paper and pasted in place, or painted with tempera paints as desired.

B. Procedure: Stuff crumpled newspaper into the toe of the sock to form a head shape. Push the stick into the center of the newspaper ball. Use black yarn to tie tightly around the neck of the puppet to hold the newspaper and stick in place (see figure 1).

Add yarn hair and a construction paper hat. Embroider, paint or paste on facial features cut from colored construction paper.

To operate the puppet, put your hand inside the sock and hold the stick (see figure 2). Crouch below a table, hold the puppet above the table and the witch is ready for action.

Example:

figure 1   figure 2

17. SQUEEZE BOTTLE SPOOKS (Shown on page 16, lower left)

A. Materials: Each of the projects described is made from a plastic squeeze bottle used for packaging fresh lemon or lime juice, or from an orange colored and shaped bottle used for packaging vitamin C tablets. Additional decorative materials are listed with each project.

B. Procedure:

1. Halloween Witch (shown on page 16): For the base of the witch use a plastic lime juice bottle (this gives the witch a lovely, sickly green complexion!). Glue on bits of scraggly black yarn hair and use tempera paints or a felt tipped pen to draw her spooky face. Cut a witch's hat from black construction paper and set the hat in place.

2. Spider (shown on page 16): Use enamel paint to paint the bottle solid black. Use a yarn needle to punch four holes along each side of the bottle. Cut four pipestem cleaners in half. Insert a length of pipestem cleaners in each of the holes, then bend the pipestem cleaners to form spider leg shapes. Use white enamel paint to add eyes to the spider. It doesn't show in the photograph, but the spider pictured on the page has a red hour glass painted on its underside to make it an authentic Black Widow!

3. Skeleton: Paint an orange plastic vitamin C bottle white, using enamel paint. When the paint has dried, use black enamel to paint the eyes, nose and mouth.

Cut two bone shapes from white construction paper or tagboard. Lay the two bones, one on top of the other, to create an "X" shape. Glue the bones together in this **position**.

Put a little glue on the bottom of the painted plastic bottle and set it on the crossed bones.

Example:

4. Bat: Use enamel paint to paint a plastic squeeze bottle solid black. When this paint has dried, use white enamel paint to add the bat's eyes and tiny, sharp teeth.

Cut two bat wings from black construction paper. Glue one wing to each side of the bat's body.

Example:

5. Black Cat: Use black enamel paint to paint an orange vitamin C bottle solid black. Allow the paint to dry thoroughly.

Cut a cat's head shape from black construction paper. Use pieces cut from colored paper and paste onto the head shape to create the cat's eyes, nose, mouth and whiskers.

Paste the head shape to the neck of the black painted bottle.

Example:

6. Ghost: Use enamel paint to paint a plastic squeeze bottle solid white. When this paint has dried, use black enamel paint to add the eyes, nose and mouth.

Set the ghost head on a small box or a plastic spray can lid. Drape a white facial tissue

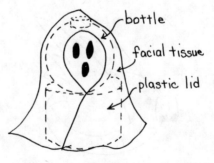

over the top of the ghost's head and tape or glue it in place like a shawl fastened around the ghost's neck. Arrange the folds of the tissue to completely cover the small box or plastic lid on which the ghost's head is resting.

7. Jack-O-Lantern (shown on page 16): A plastic vitamin C bottle is already orange colored with a green cap — perfect coloring for a jack-o-lantern and its stem.

Simply paint on a jack-o-lantern face, using either a felt pen (easiest, but the colors will smudge) or black enamel paint, or features can be cut from construction paper and glued onto the bottle.

18. PAPER SCULPTURE PUMPKIN
(Shown on page 16, lower right)

A. Materials: Construction paper, scissors, ruler, pencil and tape or staples are needed for this activity.

B. Procedure: Cut and assemble pieces for the paper sculpture pumpkin as directed below.

Example:

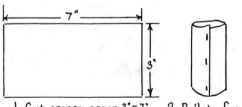

1. Cut orange paper 3"x7".

2. Roll to form a cylinder.

3. Cut green paper 3" square. Score and fold dotted lines to make valleys and solid lines to make ridges.

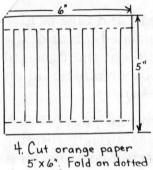

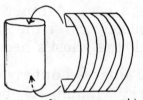

4. Cut orange paper
5"x 6". Fold on dotted
lines. Cut on solid lines.

5. Glue flaps into cylinder
to form pumpkin shape. Set
green lid on top.

19. CREPE PAPER JACK-O-LANTERN

A. Materials: Provide orange and green crepe paper, stapler or needle and thread, old newspapers and tempera paint or colored construction paper for decorating the pumpkin.

Example:

Staple open side

Tie bottom.

Fill with paper ball.

Tie top shut

Wrap stem and
decorate face.

B. Procedure: Make a "sleeve" by folding a strip of orange crepe paper in half, then stapling or sewing shut the open edge. Tie the bottom end of the sleeve together. Turn the paper inside out (to hide the seams) and fill it with a ball of wadded newspapers. Tie the top of the pumpkin shut.

Wrap green crepe paper around the pumpkin stem, then add facial features cut from construction paper or painted with tempera paints.

20. REAL PUMPKIN JACK-O-LANTERN

A. Materials: A real pumpkin, table knife, pencil, old newspapers and a spoon are needed for this activity.

B. Procedure: You'd be surprised how many students have never cut a real pumpkin to make a jack-o-lantern. And it's so easy to do!

Have each student bring a small pumpkin and a table knife from home. Spread several layers of old newspapers under the pumpkins before the students begin cutting.

First, cut out the lid of the jack-o-lantern. Using a table knife, cut a slant so the top rim of the lid will be larger in circumference than the bottom of the lid. The lid shrinks slightly as the pumpkin dries and this added width at the top prevents it from dropping down inside the pumpkin.

Use a spoon to scoop out the seeds and pulp from inside the pumpkin. (If the teacher and/or a few students have the patience, the seeds can be washed free of pulp, simmered about 2 hours in salted water, dried, then spread in a single layer in a flat pan. Add a little vegetable oil, salt and oven roast at 250° until golden. These seeds make a delicious and nutritional recess snack.)

Use a pencil to mark features on the outside of the pumpkin shell. Use a table knife to cut away sections of the pumpkin along these penciled guidelines to make eyes, ears, nose and mouth.

If desired, features may be made from other materials. For example, a long carrot may be inserted for the jack-o-lantern's nose, yarn pinned in place for hair, funny hats made of construction paper, etc.

For safety's sake (especially if flammable decorations are used), put a small flashlight rather than a candle inside the pumpkin to illuminate its features.

21. SOAP SCULPTURE JACK-O- LANTERN

A. Materials: Soap clay (recipe below), tempera paints and brushes are needed for this activity.

B. Procedure: Place in a large bowl the following ingredients:
2 cups soap flakes, soap powder or powdered detergent
½ cup water

Beat with a rotary beater until the mixture begins to stiffen. Add more soap flakes until the mixture feels firm like bread dough. If the mixture becomes too stiff to beat, stir in the extra soap with a spoon.

Have students dip their hands in cold water before working with this mixture so it will not stick to their hands.

Mold pumpkin shapes with the soap clay. Allow the figures to dry thoroughly. They can be painted orange with tempera paints. When this paint is dry use black to create the jack-o-lantern eyes, nose and mouth.

Soap clay molds nicely, but shapes begin to deteriorate after about a week. If you want these sculptures for a display, make them only a day or so before displaying.

22. JACK-O-LANTERN MOBILE

A. Materials: Students will need whole walnuts in the shell, black thread, white glue in a squeeze top bottle, felt pens or tempera paints and brushes and a stick from which to hang the jack-o-lantern faces.

B. Procedure: Squeeze a fine line of white glue along the crack in the walnut shell where the two halves meet. Lay thread firmly into the glued crack, going completely around the shell. Tie at the top, leaving a generous length of thread for suspending the shell. Let the glue dry thoroughly.

Use tempera paints or felt pens to color jack-o-lantern faces on the shell (see figure 1). Color a face on both sides of each shell so it will be equally pretty when viewed from either side.

Tie a group of the jack-o-lanterns to a stick to create a mobile (see figure 2).

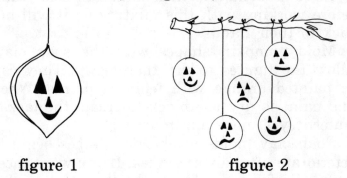

figure 1   figure 2

23. BOX-ON-BOX MASK (Shown on page 29, upper left)

A. Materials: Provide boxes of various sizes and shapes. In the photograph on page 29, a shoe box lid was used as the base of the mask. The eyes and nose are spice cans and the mouth is made from an oatmeal box lid. Brown wrapping paper (use pieces cut from old grocery sacks), masking tape, straight pins, scissors, tempera paints and brushes are also needed.

B. Procedure: Choose a flat box for the base of the mask. Cover the box with brown wrapping paper. Choose other boxes of appropriate sizes and shapes for the eyes, nose, mouth, ears, etc. Cover each of these boxes with

UPPER LEFT: Box on Box Mask
RIGHT: Paper Sculpture Mask
LOWER LEFT: Foil Faces

brown paper. Pin each box in place with straight pins or tape with masking tape. Facial details may be painted with tempera paint, cut from colored construction paper and pasted in place or simply colored with crayons if desired.

This type of mask is intended solely for display, as there are no eye holes cut and the pins used in construction would present a safety hazard.

24. PAPER SCULPTURE MASKS (Shown on page 29, right)

A. Materials: Provide colored construction paper, scissors and paste, cellophane tape and/or stapler for fastening paper pieces together.

B. Procedure: To make the basic mask shape, roll a sheet of colored paper to form a cylinder, fold the paper in half to form a single ridge line down the center of the paper, or fold

Example:

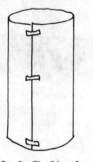 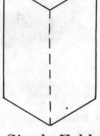 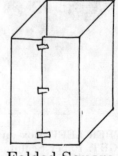

Rolled Cylinder   Single Fold   Folded Square

the paper to form a square. Tape or staple overlapped edges together. Each of these forms will stand alone for table top display.

Cut features from colored paper and paste, staple or tape them onto the main form to create hair, eyes, nose, mouth and any other desired decorations. Paper can be fringed, rolled, scored and folded, etc, to create three-dimensional effects.

25. FOIL FACES (Shown on page 29, lower left).

A. Materials: Household aluminum foil, scissors, (optionally tempera paint), brushes and soap flakes are needed for this activity

B. Procedure: Cut two sheets of aluminum foil and lay them one on top of the other to form a double thickness of foil. Place this over your face and press gently on the foil to make it fit all contours of your face. Keep your eyes shut while you do this, for sharp ridges sometimes form in the folds of the foil.

After the main facial features have been shaped in the foil, remove the mask and trim the edges of the foil into a face shape. Cut ears along each side, then fringe and roll the top for a hair-like effect.

The completed Foil Face may be left plain to resemble the famous South American tin masks, or features may be painted on with tempera paint. Add some soap flakes to the tempera paint and it will adhere to the foil surface.

26. PAPER PLATE MASK

A. Materials: Each student will need a paper plate, scissors, string and materials for decorating the mask (crayons, colored paper, yarn, tempera paint, etc.).

B. Procedure: Use a paper plate for the base of the mask. Holding the plate over a student's face, mark the placement of holes for eyes, nose and mouth. Then remove the mask and cut these holes.

Cut features from colored paper and paste them in place, paint the features with tempera paint, or simply color them with crayons. Yarn or fringed paper may be used for hair.

Tie a length of string to each side of the mask. The students may tie these strings around their heads to hold the masks in place.

Example:

27. PAPER BAG MASK

A. Materials: Each student will need a paper bag that fits over his head, scissors and materials for decorating the mask (colored construction paper, crayons, yarn, tempera paints and brushes, etc.).

B. Procedure: With the paper bag over the student's head, mark the placement of holes for eyes, nose and mouth. Remove the bag and cut these holes. Features may be colored with crayon, cut from construction paper and pasted in place, painted with tempera paints, etc.

Example:

28. PAPER STRIP MÂCHÉ MASK

A. Materials: A simple china bowl to use as a mold, liquid vegetable oil, old newspapers, string, flour, water, containers for holding paste, (disposable aluminum pie pans are perfect), scissors, sandpaper, tempera paints, brushes and (optionally) shellac are needed for this activity.

B. Procedure: Turn the bowl upside down. Grease the exposed surface with liquid vegetable oil. Place wads of paper, tied with string to maintain shape, in position on the bowl where bulges are desired for nose, ears, etc.

Cut one inch widths of newspaper. Make a runny flour and water paste. Dip one strip in paste and pull it between thumb and forefinger to remove excess paste. Lay this strip across the bowl. Continue placing strips of pasted paper across the bowl, covering the wadded paper as you work. Place two completely covering layers over the mask surface, keeping the strips as free from wrinkles as possible.

Allow the paper strips to dry completely (overnight). Remove the bowl and wadded paper from the back of the mask and trim the edges even. Add 4 to 5 additional pasted strip layers and allow the mask to dry again.

Cut the edges of the mask even and sand off any roughness on the face and edges of the mask. Paint the mask with tempera paint and add a finishing coat of shellac if desired.

29. SHOE BOX MASK

A. Materials: For each mask provide one shoe box, scissors, a length of string and materials for decorating the mask (crayons, colored construction paper, tempera paint, etc.).

B. Procedure: Cut one end from a shoe box. This cut side becomes the chin end of the mask. The opposite end of the box will rest against the top of the student's head.

Hold the box over the student's face and mark the placement of holes for eyes, nose and mouth. Remove the mask and cut these holes. Decorate the mask as desired with tempera paints, or cover the box with colored paper and paste on cut paper features, or simply color the facial features with crayons.

Punch a hole in each side of the box and tie on strings. Tie these strings around the student's head to hold the mask in place.

Example:

30. CARDBOARD LAYERED MASK

A. Materials: Provide cardboard, scissors, white glue, tempera paints and brushes.

B. Procedure: Cut the basic mask form from cardboard. Cut features such as eyes, nose, ears, hair, etc., from cardboard and glue them in place on the basic form. Build up several layers of cardboard wherever possible for greatest relief effect.

When all the glue has dried thoroughly, paint the mask with tempera paints. These masks are effective painted in one solid color, or different areas of the mask may be painted in different colors if desired.

31. PAPER BAG COSTUME

A. Materials: Students will need giant paper bags, scissors and materials for decorating the costume; such as tempera paints and brushes, crayons, colored construction paper, etc.

B. Procedure: Use as large a paper bag as can be found. Pull the bag down over the student's head and mark the placement of holes in the appropriate places for arms, eyes, nose and mouth.

Remove the bag and cut the holes as marked. Then decorate the bag with tempera paints or any other materials to create the costume desired.

Example:

32. CARDBOARD BOX COSTUMES

A. Materials: A large cardboard box, scissors, tempera paints and brushes are needed for this activity.

B. Procedure: Cut a slot about 6 inches by 3 inches on two sides of the box, close to the bottom edges. These holes will become handles by which the child may hold the box in position when it is worn as a costume.

Put the box over the student's head. As he holds the box in a comfortable position, mark the placement of a rectangular slot at eye level.

Then he may remove the box, cut out the eye-level viewing slot and paint it with tempera paints to create whatever type of costume he wishes.

Example:

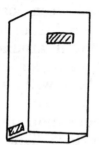

Cut slots, then decorate box.

Hold box costume like this.

33. GREASE PAINT

A. Materials: For brown grease paint you will need:

    1 tsp. solid white shortening
    2½ tsp. cocoa (unsugared)

For white grease paint you will need:

    2 tsp. solid white shortening
    5 tsp. corn starch
    1 tsp. flour
    3-4 drops glycerin

For colored grease paint use the white grease paint recipe, and add liquid food coloring, a drop at a time, to achieve the desired color.

Also needed are additional solid white shortening or cold cream and a towel to throw over the student's shoulders to protect clothing from paint smears.

B. Procedure: Safer and more realistic than masks, grease paint in any desired color may be applied directly on the student's face to create the finishing touches for a Halloween costume.

Mix desired colors of grease paint according to the recipes given. Put a towel around the student's shoulders to prevent paint smears on clothing. Coat the student's face with a thin layer of solid white shortening or cold cream. Use tissue to wipe off this application, leaving only a very thin layer on the face. This layer makes paint easier to remove later.

Use your fingers or a paintbrush to apply a thin layer of grease paint on the student's face using one or more colors as needed to achieve the desired effect.

To remove the make-up, spread solid white shortening, cold cream or baby oil over the painted areas of the face. Wipe with tissues to remove the coloring.

SECTION II:
"THANKSGIVING"

Pilgrims, Indians and turkeys are the main theme for craft projects in this chapter.

TOP: Paper Plate Turkey
BOTTOM LEFT: Paper Plate Pilgrim
BOTTOM RIGHT: Paper Plate Indian

—41—

1. PAPER PLATE TURKEY (Shown on page 41, top)

A. Materials: For each turkey you will need two pressed paper plates (paint will not adhere to wax or plastic coated plates), brown tempera paint and brushes, construction paper in a variety of colors, scissors, cellophane tape and a stapler.

B. Procedure: Paint the bottom (convex) side of two paper plates with brown tempera paint. Allow this paint to dry thoroughly.

Cut construction paper into strips 1″ wide by 12″ long. You will need 12 strips in all, in a variety of colors.

Form loops with 8 paper strips and tape these loops along the inside (eating surface) margin of one plate. Cut head and feet shapes from colored paper. Tape them in proper position to the inside margin of the plate.

Staple the two plates together, painted sides out. Cut the remaining 4 paper strips in half. Form them into loops and tape 4 loops onto each side of the paper plates to form the turkey's wings. Punch a hole at the top of the turkey's body and tie on a hanging string, if desired.

2. PAPER PLATE PILGRIM (Shown on page 41, lower left)

A. Materials: For each pilgrim figure you will need two paper plates, a stapler, tempera paints and brushes and decorative materials; such as, construction paper, fabric scraps, aluminum foil, yarn, etc.

B. Procedure: Paint the back (convex) surface of one paper plate a flesh color. This will serve as the Pilgrim's head. Paint the second plate black. This will be the Pilgrim's body. Allow the paint to dry thoroughly.

Overlap the rims of the two plates and staple them together. Then use tempera paints, construction paper, fabric scraps, yarn, etc., to add facial features, clothing details, feet, arms, etc., as desired.

3. PAPER PLATE INDIAN (Shown on page 41, lower right)

A. Materials: For each Indian figure you will need two paper plates, a stapler, tempera paints and brushes, and decorative materials; such as, construction paper, fabric scraps, yarn, etc.

B. Procedure: Paint the back (convex) side of each plate with flesh colored tempera paint. Allow the paint to dry thoroughly.

Overlap the rims of the two plates and staple them together. The plate at the top will be the Indian's head and the plate below will be the body.

Use tempera paints, construction paper, fabric, yarn, etc., to add facial features, hair, clothing, arms, feet, etc., as desired.

4. PINE CONE TURKEY

A. Materials: Students will need pine cones, construction paper, scissors, tempera paint or crayons and glue.

B. Procedure: The pine cone forms the base for this turkey. Cut head and tail shapes from construction paper. Decorate them as desired with crayons or tempera paint. Glue the paper tail to the wide, flat end of the pine cone, and the paper head to the narrow end.

Example:

5. TURNIP LANTERN

A. Materials: For each lantern you will need a turnip (a white or sweet potato could be used instead), a sharp knife, a spoon, a nail, wire, a candle and a sturdy stick.

B. Procedure: In Switzerland, the Netherlands and Germany, children celebrate the harvest season by parading through the streets carrying lanterns made from vegetables, just as children in America carry lighted pumpkins for Halloween.

To make a turnip lantern, use a sharp knife to cut the flat top off a turnip (or potato). Use a spoon to scoop out the interior portion, leaving smooth walls. Use a knife to carve designs in the sides of the walls. Designs can be carved all the way through the sides, or only partway. Partially cut designs allow a transparent glow of light to show through.

Use a nail to punch two holes, directly across from each other, near the top of the walls. Insert wire through these holes to form a hanging loop. Securely fasten the hanging loop to a stick. Put a candle in the lantern, light it and carry it by the stick handle.

Example:

6. SPLIT PAPER CORNUCOPIA (Shown on page 46, top)

A. Materials: Provide construction paper, ruler, pencil, scissors and stapler. Fill the cornucopia with artificial fruit, or fruit pieces made from clay or papier mâché.

TOP: Split Paper Cornucopia
CENTER LEFT: Walnut Shell Turkey
CENTER RIGHT: Potato Turkey
BOTTOM: Pilgrim Ships (3 examples)

B. Procedure: Cut a sheet of 9″ x 12″ construction paper as shown below in figure 1. Overlap corner number 1 with corner 2 (as shown in figure 2) and tape or staple in place to form the cornucopia shape. Fill with artificial fruits and/or vegetables.

Example:

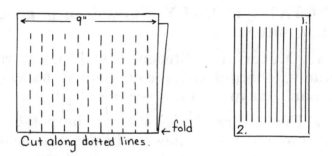

figure 1   figure 2

7. WALNUT SHELL TURKEY (Shown on page 46, left center)

A. Materials: A walnut, knife, construction paper, scissors, crayons or felt pens, a rubber band and white glue are needed for this activity.

B. Procedure: Slip the tip of a knife blade into the crack between the two halves of the walnut shell. Turn the blade to pry open the shell. This method produces two perfect, unbroken shell halves. Remove the nut meat.

Cut a turkey head, tail and leg shapes from construction paper. Use crayons or felt pens to add any desired decorations to these paper shapes.

Apply glue to the rims of both halves of the walnut shell. Put the two halves together inserting the turkey head, tail and leg pieces in proper position between the shells. Put a rubber band around the completed construction to hold it firmly together while the glue dries. Remove the rubber band when the glue is dry.

8. POTATO TURKEY (Shown on page 46, right center)

A. Materials: Students will need raw potatoes, sharp knives, construction paper or tagboard, crayons and scissors.

B. Procedure: Make slits in the potato as shown by the dotted lines in the example below. From construction paper or tagboard, cut pieces for the turkey's head, tail and wings as shown. Decorate the pieces with crayoned details.

Fit the head, tail and wing pieces into the slits to complete the turkey form.

Example:

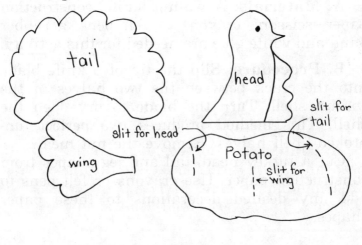

9. PILGRIM SHIPS (Shown at the bottom of page 46)

A. Materials: Provide whole walnuts, knives, clay, toothpicks, white construction paper and scissors.

B. Procedure: Half a walnut shell forms the hull of the ship. To open the walnuts, slip the tip of a knife blade into the crack between the two shell halves. Turn the blade to pry open the shell. It will split into two perfect, unbroken halves.

Place a small ball of clay in the bottom of the shell and use this to anchor an upright toothpick mast. Sails are cut from white construction paper and simply threaded onto the toothpick mast.

Example:

10. ENGLISH CORN DOLLY

A. Materials: For each corn doll you will need an ear of corn complete with husks, yarn or string, pins or glue, oil base paint (a small jar of model paint works well) and a paintbrush.

B. Procedure: An English custom is to save one ear of corn from one harvest to the next. This ear symbolizes the spirit of the corn goddess, passing hope for a fruitful harvest to the next season. The corn is made into the shape of a woman.

First peel back the leaves halfway down the ear as shown in figure 1. Tie string or yarn **over** the front and back husk sections (holding them flat against the ear), and **under** the side husk sections (so they can stand out to form arms) as shown in figure 2.

Pull side leaves so they stand out straight from the ear. Tie yarn around the ends of these two sections to create the doll's hands. Pin or glue on yarn hair and paint on facial features, as shown in figure 3.

Example:

figure 1   figure 2   figure 3

11. INDIAN CORN DOLL

A. Materials: For each Indian figure you will need an ear of corn with husks, plus decorative materials as suggested.

B. Procedure: Peel the leaves about halfway down the ear. Tie string around the top edge of the leaves to hold them firmly against the ear.

Use enamel paint to paint facial features on the ear. Pin on yarn hair and make a cut paper headband with feathers. Add any decorative features desired.

Example:

12. PAPER BAG TURKEY (Shown on page 52, top)

A. Materials: Provide a lunch-size paper bag, old newspapers, string, colored construction paper, scissors, felt pens or crayons and glue, tape and/or a stapler.

B. Procedure: Fill the bag about 2/3 full of crumpled newspapers. Tie the bag tightly shut against the stuffing and fan out the open end of the bag as shown in figure 1.

Cut large feather shapes from construction paper and staple them to the open end of the sack to form the turkey's tail.

TOP: Paper Bag Turkey
CENTER: Hand Pattern Turkey (2 examples)
LOWER LEFT: Paper Sculpture Turkey
LOWER RIGHT: Paper Tube Turkeys (3 examples)

Cut smaller feather shapes and glue or tape them to the sides of the bag to form wings.

Cut two turkey head shapes from construction paper, adding tabs where the neck will meet the body, as shown in figure 2. Decorate both head pieces with felt pen or crayoned facial details. Glue the front portion of the two heads together, spread apart the tab ends and glue or tape these tabs onto the bag as shown in figure 3.

Example:

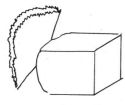
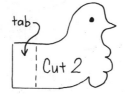

figure 1   figure 2   figure 3

13. HAND PATTERN TURKEY (Shown on page 52, center)

A. Materials: Construction paper, pencil, scissors and crayons (or tempera paints and brushes) are needed for this activity.

B. Procedure: Have a student place one hand, with thumb outstreched and fingers slightly spread, on a sheet of construction paper. He may use a pencil to trace around the shapes of his hand.

Using the traced hand shape as the basic turkey form, have him **sketch** in freehand the turkey's head, wattle and feet as shown.

Then he may cut out the turkey and decorate it with crayons or tempera paint.

Example:

14. PAPER SCULPTURE TURKEY
(Shown on page 52, lower left)

A. Materials: Students will need construction paper, scissors and a stapler.

B. Procedure: Cut and fold paper as directed below to form the turkey. The bottom of the feet may be folded out and stapled **or** taped

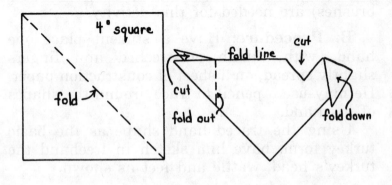

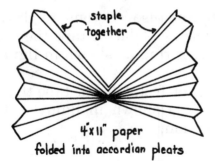

staple together

4"x11" paper
folded into accordian pleats

staple tail to turkey body

to a sheet of paper so the bird will stand erect. The bottom edge may be fitted into slots in a place card to be used as a party decoration.

15. PAPER TUBE TURKEY (Shown on page 52, lower right)

A. Materials: Provide cardboard tubes from paper towel rolls, scissors, colored construction paper, crayons, glue and tape.

B. Procedure: Cut a ring of cardboard tubing about 1½" wide. Cut a strip of colored construction paper 1½" wide and long enough to wrap around the cardboard ring with some overlap. Tape the strip around the ring.

Cut a strip of construction paper about 1" wide and 3" long. Roll it to form a ring and tape ends securely together. This will be the turkey's head. From colored paper, cut and fasten on the beak and wattle pieces. Use crayons to color the turkey's eyes. Tape or glue the head to the body as shown in figure 1.

Cut two colored paper wing shapes and tape them to the interior of the larger ring as shown in figure 2.

Cut a paper tail and use crayons to draw multi-colored feather strips. Glue or tape the tail to the back of the larger ring as shown in figure 3.

Cut two colored paper feet. Glue or tape them under the larger ring, as shown in figure 4, to complete the construction.

Example:

figure 1 figure 2

figure 3 figure 4

16. INDIAN CHIEF HEADDRESS

A. Materials: Each student will need a paper bag that fits snugly around his head, scissors and tempera paints or crayons for decorating the headdress.

B. Procedure: Cut the bottom off the paper bag. Lay the remaining portion flat, as shown in figure 1. Fold the bag in half as shown in figure 2. Then fold it in half again as shown in figure 3.

Example:

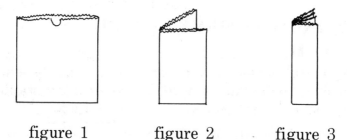

figure 1   figure 2   figure 3

Leaving about a 2 inch wide strip at the bottom to serve as the headband, draw and cut out a feather shape in the upper part of the folded bag as shown in figure 4.

Open up the headdress. Fold the headband strip in half, lengthwise, as shown in figure 5. This gives double strength to the band. Then use crayons, tempera paint, felt tipped pens or any other desired materials to decorate the feathers and headdress as shown in figure 6.

Example:

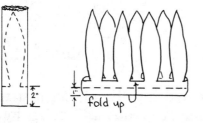
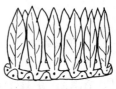

figure 4   figure 5   figure 6

Finally, make a firmly creased vertical fold along the center line of each feather. This adds strength to the paper so the feathers will stand erect.

17. INDIAN BRAVE COSTUME

A. Materials: Brown paper grocery bags, tagboard, scissors, tempera paint and brushes (or crayons could be used, if preferred), a stapler and string are needed for this activity.

B. Procedure: To make the Indian's "deerskin" vest, cut a large brown grocery bag up the center and cut away shaded areas for neck and arm holes as shown in figure 1, below.

Use tempera paints or crayons to decorate the vest with Indian designs as desired. Cut closely spaced slits about 3″ long around the lower edge of the vest to represent fringe (see figure 2).

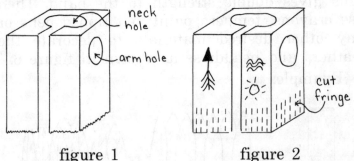

figure 1   figure 2

To make a feathered headband, cut a strip of brown wrapping paper about 24″ long by 2″ wide. Fold the band in half, lengthwise, for greater strength. Use tempera paints or crayons to color Indian symbols on the band. Cut one or more feather shapes from tagboard (or use real feathers, if available). Color the feathers as desired, then staple or tape them to the inside of the headband. Overlap the headband ends. Hold the ends in position around the student's head to make sure the band fits snugly. Then remove the band from his head and staple the overlapped ends in place.

Example:

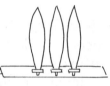

Headband (double thickness)   Feathers taped to back side   Ends overlapped and stapled to form headband.

To make a breechcloth, cut two rectangles from brown wrapping paper, each about 12″ square. Cut a 36 inch length of string.

Fold the top edge of each brown paper square over the string and staple through the double thickness of paper. Decorate the front side of each breechcloth section with Indian designs. Cut fringe along the bottom edge of each piece as described in directions for the Indian vest above.

Tie the string around the student's waist and move the breechcloth sections so one hangs at his center front, the other at his center back.

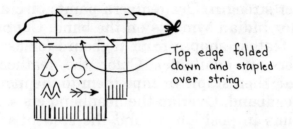

Top edge folded down and stapled over string.

18. INDIAN MAIDEN COSTUME

A. Materials: Brown grocery bags, tempera paint and brushes and scissors are needed for this activity.

B. Procedure: For the Indian Maiden's wig, select a brown grocery sack that fits over the student's head comfortably and extends down to about shoulder level or longer. Paint the entire exterior surface of the bag with black tempera paint and allow this paint to dry thoroughly.

Cut the sides of the bag into slender strips, beginning at the open end of the bag and extending almost to the bottom edge of the bag (see figure 1).

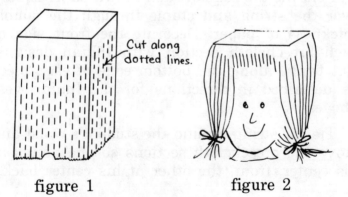

Cut along dotted lines.

figure 1   figure 2

—60—

On the front side of the bag cut off center strips to leave about 2½″ lengths to create bangs. Gather all remaining strips into two bundles, one on each side of the bag, and tie them with string or yarn to form braid shapes (see figure 2).

To complete the costume, make a feathered headband and "deerskin" vest as described in "Indian Brave Costume", page 58.

19. PILGRIM MAN'S COSTUME

A. Materials: Provide white and black construction paper, household aluminum foil, scissors, glue and a stapler.

B. Procedure: For the collar, begin with a 15″ x 18″ rectangle of white construction paper. Trim the corners to form an oval shape and cut away the center, shaded as shown in the example below.

Example:

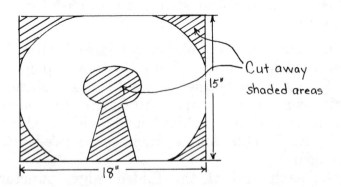

For the hat band cut a strip of black construction paper about 1½" wide and long enough to fit around the child's head with an inch or two of overlap. Cut a rectangle of black construction paper about 9" x 6" in size. From household aluminum foil, cut shapes for the hat band and buckle. Glue these foil pieces onto the black rectangle as shown in figure 1. Staple the hat band onto the hat as shown in figure 2. Staple the strip ends together to complete the construction as shown in figure 3.

Example:

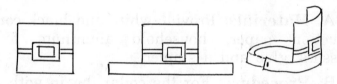

figure 1   figure 2   figure 3

20. PILGRIM WOMAN'S COSTUME

A. Materials: White construction paper, scissors, stapler and string are needed for this activity.

B. Procedure: Make a white collar as described in "Pilgrim Man's Costume", page 61.

To make the bonnet, use a 12" x 18" sheet of white construction paper. Along one 18" side of the sheet fold up a strip about 1" wide as shown in figure 1. This double thickness is needed for strength.

At each end of the folded edge, puncture holes and tie on bonnet strings as shown in figure 2. You may wish to reinforce the punctured holes with paper reinforcers or squares of cellophane tape to keep the string from tearing through the paper.

Cut along dotted lines as shown in figure 2. Bring the two outer edge points marked "X" to overlap the center point marked "y", and staple through all three thicknesses of paper.

Tie bonnet strings under the chin to hold the hat in place.

Example:

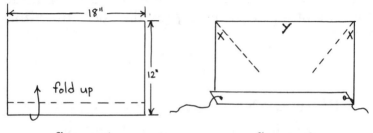

figure 1   figure 2

21. SUET BLOCK BIRD FEEDER

A. Materials: For each block you will need about one pound of suet, 1½ cups of birdseed, a covered fry pan, hot plate, a one quart milk carton and string or yarn.

B. Procedure: A suet block provides a thoughtful Thanksgiving feast for the birds. Slice the suet into tiny pieces and put them in a frying pan. Cover the pan (to protect from splatters) and set the heat VERY LOW.

When almost all of the suet has melted, remove the pan from the heat and allow it to cool for about half an hour. Stir in the birdseed and allow the mixture to cool about one hour.

Then spoon the mixture into a milk carton to cool and solidify completely (refrigerate overnight if possible).

Peel away the paper carton, tie string around the suet and hang the block from a tree limb.

C. Variation: In place of part or all of the birdseed, use cornmeal, rolled oats, crushed breadcrumbs, cracker crumbs or any similar ingredients that would provide good nutrition for the birds.

22. PINE CONE BIRD FEEDER

A. Materials: Pine cones with widely-opened petals, thin wire, paper towels and a mixture of 1 cup peanut butter, 2—3 cups wild birdseed and 3 cups finely ground or chopped suet.

B. Procedure: Firmly wrap wire around the top few petals of the pine cone, making a loop about 6″ long extending above the pine cone top. This wire loop will be used for hanging the completed feeder.

Thoroughly mix the peanut butter, birdseed and suet. Use your fingers to pack this mixture into the spaces between the pine cone petals. Only the tips of the petals will show when this step is completed. The mixture is gooey, so keep lots of paper towels handy for wiping off hands.

Hang the feeder from a tree branch and watch the birds enjoy this Thanksgiving feast.

You can make many of these feeders, wrap them in plastic wrap or foil, then refrigerate or freeze them to save for future use.

SECTION III:
"CHRISTMAS"

A wide array of craft projects are designed to help students express the joy and beauty of this happy holiday season.

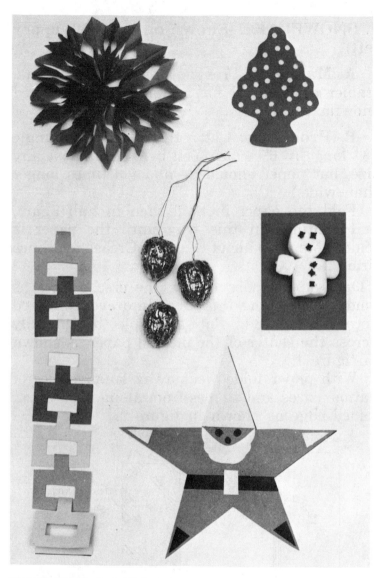

UPPER LEFT: Snowflake
UPPER RIGHT: "Lighted" Tree
LOWER LEFT: Chain Garland
CENTER: Walnut Sparkles
RIGHT CENTER: Marshmallow Snowman
LOWER RIGHT: Star Santa

1. SNOWFLAKE (Shown on page 69, upper left)

A. Materials: Provide tissue paper, scissors, stapler and thread for hanging the completed snowflakes.

B. Procedure: Cut a tissue paper rectangle 18″ long by 6″ wide. (You can use almost any size, but paper should be about 3 times longer than wide.)

Fold the paper in half, then in half again, and continue in this way until the paper is folded to a strip about ½″ wide. Crease fold lines firmly.

Open up the tissue. Use the crease lines as guides for folding the paper into evenly-spaced accordian pleats. Put a staple horizontally across the center of the pleated paper as shown in figure 1.

With paper folded, cut away small pieces of various sizes and shapes from along each outer, folded edge as shown in figure 2.

Example:

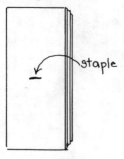

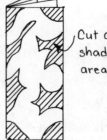

Cut away shaded areas.

Figure 1   Figure 2

Fan out the pleats to form a full circle and staple edges from the portion above the center staple to the portion below the staple. Tie a hanging thread through one of the cut-outs near the top edge of the snowflake.

2. "LIGHTED" TREE (Shown on page 69, upper right)

A. Materials: Provide construction paper, colored tissue paper or colored cellophane, scissors, a paper punch and paste.

B. Procedure: Cut two identical Christmas tree shapes from construction paper and the same shape from colored tissue paper or cellophane. Place the two construction paper shapes one on top of the other, and punch holes here and there with a paper punch to represent lights. Sandwich the tissue paper or cellophane tree between the two construction paper trees and paste the three shapes together.

Display the tree on a window pane, where the light shining through makes it appear to be gaily lighted. The tree is equally pretty when viewed from either side of the glass.

3. CHAIN GARLAND (Shown on page 69, lower left.)

A. Materials: Colored paper, ruler, pencil and scissors are needed for this activity.

B. Procedure: Cut many 2″ x 4″ rectangles of paper. Fold each paper in half to form a 2″ square.

Draw and cut out links in any desired shape from folded paper as shown in figure 1. Open one link and slip half through a folded link. Refold this second link. Open a third link, slip half through the second link and refold the third link (see figure 2). Continue in this way to make a chain of any desired length.

Example:

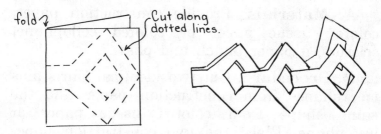

figure 1   figure 2

4. WALNUT SPARKLES (Shown on page 69, center)

A. Materials: Whole walnuts, black thread, white glue in a squeeze-top bottle, gold paint, brushes and gold glitter are needed for this activity.

B. Procedure: Squeeze a fine line of white glue along the crack where the two halves of a walnut shell meet. Lay thread firmly into the glued crack, going completely around the shell. Tie at the top, leaving a generous length of thread at the top for tying the completed ornament onto the Christmas tree. Allow glue to dry thoroughly before proceeding.

Paint the entire walnut shell with gold paint. While the paint is still wet, sprinkle on gold glitter. Hang the ornament and allow the paint to dry thoroughly.

5. MARSHMALLOW SNOWMAN (Shown on page 69, right center)

A. Materials: For each snowman you will need 2 large marshmallows, 2 miniature marshmallows, 2 toothpicks and 5 whole cloves.

B. Procedure: Press stem ends of 3 whole cloves into the flat side of one large marshmallow to form the snowman's eyes and mouth. Set the second large marshmallow flat side down. Press stem ends of 2 whole cloves into the rounded side of this marshmallow to make the snowman's buttons.

Set the head on the body. Push a toothpick down through the two marshmallows to hold them together, as shown in figure 1.

Break a toothpick in half. Use the halves to fasten a miniature marshmallow to each side of the body, as shown in figure 2, to form the snowman's arms.

Example:

figure 1

figure 2

6. STAR SANTA (Shown on page 69, lower right)

A. Materials: Students will need red, black and white construction paper, scissors, glue and black thread for hanging the Santa. For very young children you may wish to make several 5-pointed star patterns from tagboard which they can use to trace the basic shapes.

B. Procedure: Cut a 5 pointed star from red construction paper. Lay white paper under the top point and trace the shape. Cut out this triangle and paste it on top of the point to make Santa's white hat.

Cut two small white paper triangles and fasten them to the next two points to make Santa's mittens. Cut two small black triangles and paste them to the lower 2 points to represent boots.

Cut out and paste on a black strip for a belt and a small white square for the buckle. Paste on two black circles for Santa's eyes, a tiny white circle for his nose and add a beard shape cut from white paper.

Punch a tiny hole near the top of the upper point. Tie on a hanging thread.

7. SODA STRAW CHAIN

A. Materials: Students will need soda straws (colored cellophane straws are especially effective), thread, needle, construction paper and scissors.

B. Procedure: Cut colored soda straws into one-inch lengths. Cut small shapes of stars, Christmas trees, bells or other appropriate designs from colored construction paper.

Using a needle and thread, alternately string lengths of the soda straw and colored decorations to form a chain of the desired length.

Example:

8. FLUFF ORNAMENTS

A. Materials: Provide thin paper (tissue or typing paper work well), scissors, stapler, needle and thread.

B. Procedure: Cut 6 to 12 identical paper shapes, such as circles, stars, bells, Christmas trees, etc. Shapes should be relatively small, 2-4 inches at the widest point, for you must be able to reach the center line with a stapler. Fold each shape vertically through the center.

Stack all shapes. Staple along the center line as shown in figure 1. Fan out the layers to form a complete circle. Thread a hanging loop through the top of the ornament as shown in figure 2.

Example:

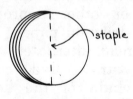

figure 1   figure 2

9. PAPER STRIP BALL

A. Materials: Colored construction paper, thread, a paper cutter and a stapler are needed for this activity.

B. Procedure: Cut three paper strips, each ½″ x 9″. (A paper cutter makes fast work of cutting 9″ x 12″ paper crosswise into ½″-wide strips. Cut through several sheets at once and you will have plenty of strips for the entire class in no time at all.) Lay the three strips as shown in figure 1 below and staple at the center crossing.

Example:

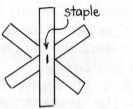  

figure 1   figure 2   figure 3

Bring ends of the top strip to overlap and form a loop. Staple the overlapped ends together as shown in figure 2. Do the same with the other two strips and tie a hanging loop of thread around the top center of the completed ball as shown in figure 3.

10. SODA STRAW SUNBURST (Shown on page 78, top center)

A. Materials: Students will need soda straws (colored cellophane straws are particularly attractive), scissors and black thread.

B. Procedure: Cut four to six soda straws in half. Holding them together to form a bundle, tie black thread tightly around the center of the bunch. Fan out the straws to form a circular, sunburst shape. Suspend the ornament from the tree by a black thread.

Example:

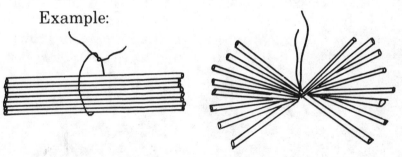

11. PAPER BIRD — Type 1 (Shown on page 78, upper right).

A. Materials: Students will need construction paper, scissors, stapler and decorative materials.

CLOCKWISE FROM TOP CENTER: Soda Straw Sunburst, Paper
Bird, Cookie Cut-Outs, Toothpick Star, Three Dimension Orna-
ment, Egg Carton Bells
CENTER: Paper Balls

B. Procedure: Cut the bird body from construction paper as shown in the pattern below. Rectangles of paper, folded into accordian pleats, make the bird's wings and tail. Slip the larger piece through the slot on the bird's back. Open up the pleats and staple edges together over the bird's back to form wings. Do the same with the smaller pleated strip to form the bird's tail.

Example:

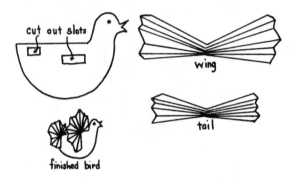

12. PAPER BIRD — Type 2

A. Materials: Construction paper and scissors are needed for this activity.

B. Procedure: Cut a pattern similar to that shown in the example. Cut wing and tail slits as shown by dotted lines, then cut away and remove the triangle-shaped piece between the wings and tail.

The fold line is not cut, except the small semi-circle cut away to form the bird's eye and the slant which forms the bird's open beak.

The bird may be opened up and decorated as desired. Gilt paint, glitter, sequins, etc., may be used. Suspend the bird from the tree with black thread, or use it as a colorful package decoration.

Example:

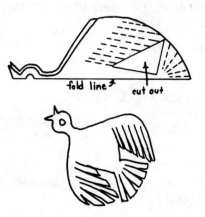

13. COOKIE CUT-OUTS (Shown on page 78, right center)

A. Materials: Self-hardening clay, smooth washable work surface, rolling pin or jar with straight sides, table knife, cookie cutters, tempera paints and heavy black thread are needed for this activity. Clear shellac is optional.

B. Procedure: Place the clay on a smooth washable surface. Use a rolling pin or the side of a glass jar to roll the clay about ¼″ thick. Use actual cookie cutters to stamp shapes on the surface of the clay, then use a table knife to cut along the indented guidelines. Punch a hole at the top of each shape.

Allow the clay to dry thoroughly. Then paint both sides of the clay shapes to resemble Christmas cookies. A finishing coat of shellac provides a shiny, durable finish.

Tie heavy black thread through the hole in the top of each cookie and hang it from the tree.

C. Variations:

1. A simpler version of the cookie decoration is to trace cookie cutter shapes on colored construction paper. Cut out the shapes and decorate them with crayons, felt pens, tempera paint or pieces cut from colored paper and pasted in place.

2. Trace cookie cutter shapes onto pieces of aluminum cut from the smooth, bottom section of disposable pans. Cut out the shapes. To decorate, brush on a thin line of white glue, then **sprinkle sparkle onto the glue, or paint the shapes with high gloss enamel paint for a truly elegant look.**

14. TOOTHPICK STAR (Shown on page 78, lower right)

A. Materials: Provide aluminum foil, colored toothpicks and black thread.

B. Procedure: Mold a piece of aluminum foil into a tight ball about the size of a walnut. Push colored toothpicks into the foil ball to form a star pattern. Suspend the star with black thread.

15. THREE-DIMENSIONAL ORNAMENTS
(Shown on page 78, bottom center)

A. Materials: Provide construction paper, scissors and black thread.

B. Procedure: Cut two identical shapes from construction paper. Cut a slit in each, as shown below. Fit the two shapes together, fitting one slit down onto the other. Hang the ornament with black thread.

Example:

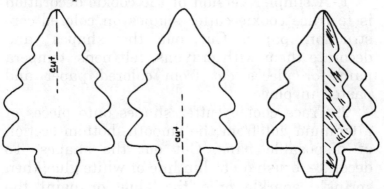

16. EGG CARTON BELLS (Shown on page 78, left)

A. Materials: Provide pressed paper egg cartons, scissors, tempera paints and brushes, and thread or ribbon.

B. Procedure: Cut apart a paper egg carton to make 12 individual cups. Each cup will make one bell. Cut the edge of each cup in a scalloped, notched or smooth pattern. Paint the bells with tempera paints, painting both the inside and outside of each bell. Tiny clappers may be made from aluminum foil balls hung with black thread inside each bell.

The bells may be hung in clustered groups on bright ribbons as shown in the photograph on page 78, or hung individually.

17. PAPER BALLS (Shown on page 78, center)

A. Materials: Foil covered gift wrapping paper, scissors and black thread are needed for this activity.

B. Procedure: Cut a four-inch square of foil paper. Fold and cut the square as shown below. Notice the cut on the far right goes all the way across the paper to round off the lower right corner. But all other cuts stop just short of the far edge of the paper, with three slits cut on one side of the cone, and two on the other.

Example:

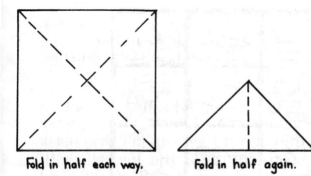

Fold in half each way.   Fold in half again.   Cut on dotted lines

Fold in half each way. Fold in half again. Cut on dotted lines.

Open the ball, fluff it out, and paste the four outside loops together to form a lacy ball. These balls may be hung singly, or in groups as shown in the photograph on page 78. They may be used as package decorations as well as tree ornaments.

18. TOY STORE WINDOW

A. Materials: Provide a large bulletin board, black and white construction paper for window frames and snow, plus scissors, pins and materials for making the toys. The toys can be drawn on manilla paper with crayons, made from construction paper scraps, or painted on brown wrapping paper with tempera paint.

B. Procedure: Cut thin strips of black construction paper and pin them in place on a large bulletin board to form a window pane pattern. Cut snow shapes from white paper and pin them in the window corners.

Have each child draw and cut out the shape of a toy he would like to have for Christmas, using any of the materials listed. Pin one toy in each section of the toy store window.

19. STAINED GLASS WINDOW

A. Materials: Students will need white scouring powder, water, tempera paints, brushes and disposable pans or cans in which to mix the colors. Designs are painted directly on the classroom windows.

B. Procedure: Mix a thick paste of white scouring powder and water. Make many batches and add a different color of dry tempera powder to each batch so there will be a variety of colors to use. Make one batch black.

Paint with this colored mixture right on the classroom windows. Apply black paint first to outline the patterns for the "lead", then fill in areas with colors as desired.

20. STARCHED STRING BALLS

A. Materials: Provide small, round balloons, flour, water, containers for paste (disposable aluminum pans work well) and heavy cotton string or cord.

B. Procedure: Mix flour and water to make a paste a little thicker than heavy cream. Blow up a small, round balloon. Dip string into the paste to saturate it thoroughly, then pull it between thumb and forefinger to remove excess paste. Wrap it around the balloon. Do not cover the balloon entirely with string, but form a lacy pattern of loops on the balloon surface.

When the paste has dried, pop the balloon and remove it from inside the ball. The string will be stiff and maintain its shape. To decorate the ball, sparingly brush on white glue and sprinkle glitter into the glue.

21. CRECHE (Shown below)

A. Materials: Provide self-hardening clay, tempera paint and brushes, a cardboard box and scissors.

Creche

B. Procedure: Cut and paint a cardboard box to make the stable, as shown. Model individual figures from clay. Allow clay to dry thoroughly, then paint with tempera paints. Assemble stable and figures to form the creche scene.

22. PICTURE FRAME SCENE

A. Materials: Students will need round or oval flat tin cans with lids removed (tuna fish, sardine or cat food cans work well), enamel paint, brushes, ribbon, glue, scissors and colored construction paper.

B. Procedure: Paint the entire inside and the outside edges of the can with enamel paint. Allow paint to dry thoroughly.

Cut needed figures from construction paper and decorate with crayons or cut paper pieces. Put a tab at the base of each piece to be bent back and used for fastening the figure in the scene.

Example:

Glue or tape the figures in place inside the can to create the desired scene. Glue or tape a ribbon to the back of the can to serve as a hanger.

23. GLITTERY PINE CONE TREE

A. Materials: Students will need pine cones, white glue and gold glitter.

B. Procedure: Brush white glue onto some of the petals of the pine cone. Sprinkle glitter onto the cone, then shake it to remove excess glitter. If work is done over a piece of paper, the glitter that falls off may be gathered into the center of the sheet and poured back into the container for future use.

These miniature, shining trees make pretty package trimmings, tree ornaments, or may be used as individual place decorations for a classroom party.

24. PAPER PLATE DOVE (Shown on page 89, upper left)

A. Materials: Very thin paper plates, scissors and crayons are needed for this activity.

B. Procedure: Mark a large crayoned dot in the very center of the paper plate. This dot will be the dove's eye. Using the eye as a point of reference, draw the bird's head. Then draw all other lines as shown in the example.

TOP: Paper Plate Dove, Christmas Sprites (2 examples)
CENTER: Three Wise Men
LOWER LEFT: Apple Santa
LOWER RIGHT: Candy Candlestick

Cut along all dotted lines. Pass ends marked "A" past each other and push slot B into slot C.

Example:

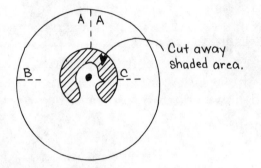

Cut away shaded area.

25. CHRISTMAS SPRITES (Shown on page 89, upper right)

A. Materials: Red and white construction paper, compass, scissors and glue are needed for this activity.

B. Procedure: These amusing sprites are a stylized version of the Scandinavian *tomte*, or Christmas elf used as table decorations, tree ornaments or to decorate gift boxes.

Cut a circle 10″ in diameter from red construction paper. Cut the circle in thirds. Roll one of these three sections to form a slender cone. (The two leftover portions of the circle can be used to make two additional sprites.) Staple the overlapped edges. Cut off about ½″ from the tip of the cone (see figure 1).

Cut a circle 5″ in diameter from white construction paper. Cut this circle in thirds. Roll one section to form a cone and staple the overlapped edges.

Put a little glue around the snipped-off top of the red cone. Put the pointed end of the white cone into the red cone as shown in figure 2. This completes the body and head of the sprite.

Cut a circle 7½″ in diameter from red construction paper. Again cut this circle in thirds. Roll one section into a cone and fasten overlapping edges. Spread white glue around the top edge of the white cone. Set the new red cone, open end down, on top to make the sprite's hat.

Example:

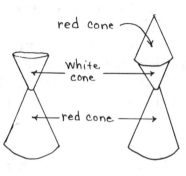

red cone

white cone

red cone

figure 1   figure 2   figure 3

Sprites can be made taller or shorter by cutting circles of larger or smaller diameters. To keep proper proportions, the white circle used for the head should be one-half the diameter of the base cone. The circle used for the hat should be three-fourths the diameter of the base cone.

To make sprites more slender, use less than one-third of the whole circle for each cone. To make sprites fatter, use more than one-third of the whole circle for each cone.

26. THREE WISE MEN (Shown on page 89, center)

A. Materials: For each set of three wise men you will need three nail polish bottles, scraps of felt, fabric or colored construction paper, white glue, scissors, and any other desired decorative materials such as gold cord, glass "jewels", sequins, etc.

B. Procedure: Each nail polish bottle forms the base for one wise man. The tall lid becomes the hat and head, the glass portion of the bottle the body. Wrap fabric or construction paper pieces around the hat and body. Cut a circle shape, decorate with facial features, and glue in place to form the head. Add capes, regal robes, "jeweled" crowns, etc., as desired.

27. APPLE SANTA (Shown on page 89, lower left)

A. Materials: For each Santa you will need a red apple, a large marshmallow, 5 whole cloves, 1 raisin or red cinnamon-candy, red construction paper, scissors, glue and white yarn or bits of cotton batting.

B. Procedure: Press 2 whole cloves into the rounded side of the marshmallow to make Santa's eyes. Glue on a red cinnamon candy or raisin for his mouth. Spread glue on the flat, bottom side of the marshmallow and set it on the apple. Press 3 cloves into the apple to represent buttons.

To make Santa's hat cut a 3″ circle of red construction paper. Cut the circle in half. Roll one half to form a cone and tape overlapped edges. Glue white yarn or cotton batting trim around the base and tip of the cone.

Spread white glue around the base of the cone and set it in place on Santa's head to complete the construction.

28. CANDY CANDLESTICK (Shown on page 89, lower right)

A. Materials: For each tiny candlestick you will need one large red or green gumdrop, one Life Saver candy and one small birthday candle.

B. Procedure: Cut a vertical slit in the upper edge of the gumdrop. Press the Life Saver into this slit, leaving about 3/4 exposed. This makes the candlestick handle.

Press a birthday candle into the center top of the gumdrop to complete the construction. (If the gumdrop is very firm, you may need to press a nail down into the top of the gumdrop to form a hole for the candle.)

29. TISSUE PAPER WREATH (Shown on page 94, top)

A. Materials: For each wreath you will need a wire coat hanger, one package of tissue paper (approximately), and a ribbon bow and/or glass ornaments for decorations.

TOP: Tissue Paper Wreath
LEFT: Macaroni Tree
RIGHT: Paper Angel

B. Procedure: Open the lower portion of the wire coat hanger to form a circle. Cut tissue paper into rectangles about 6 inches by 2½-3 inches. The wreath requires approximately one entire package of tissue paper. To speed the cutting of these rectangles, leave the paper folded as it comes in the package and cut the whole package at once into 6 inch slices with a paper cutter. Cut each slice into 3 inch segments. In this way the whole package can be cut into rectangles in just a few minutes.

Twist one rectangle in the center, as shown in step 1. Lay this twist under the wire of the hanger. Reverse the ends of the paper by passing end 1 over the wire into position beside end 2, then passing end 2 over the wire into the position end 1 has just "vacated", as shown in step 2.

Push this paper up against the neck of the hanger, and continue adding more tissue paper strips in the same way. The pressure of one strip packed tightly against the next will hold the paper in place — no glue or other fasteners are

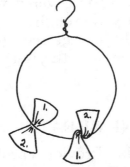

Step 1   Step 2

needed. Keep the ends turned in various directions so the wreath is equally fluffy on all sides.

When finished, add a ribbon bow to the hanger neck, and tie a few glass ornaments here and there on the wreath if desired.

30. PINE CONE WREATH

A. Materials: Cardboard, scissors, ribbon, stapler, white glue, a large ribbon bow and a large quantity of small pine cones are needed for this activity.

B. Procedure: Cut a circle from heavy cardboard. Cut away a circle from the center so the cardboard forms a wreath shape. Staple a ribbon loop to the back of the cardboard to serve as a hanger.

Paint an area of this cardboard wreath with a generous amount of white glue. Press pine cones in place, large flat end down, to fill the glued area. Continue gluing and pasting one small area at a time until the entire surface of the cardboard ring is covered with pine cones. Allow glue to dry thoroughly.

If desired, add a large red bow, wired to one pine cone, to complete the wreath.

31. MACARONI WREATH

A. Materials: Provide cardboard, scissors, white glue, raw macaroni in a variety of shapes, and gold, bronze or silver paint.

B. Procedure: Cut a wreath shape from cardboard. Staple a ribbon loop to the back of the wreath to serve as a hanger. Spread white glue over one small area of the face of the wreath. Set in raw macaroni pieces to completely cover the glued area.

Continue in this way until the entire surface of the wreath is covered with macaroni pieces. When the glue has thoroughly dried, paint the wreath with gold, bronze or silver paint. Add a bright red ribbon bow, if desired.

The picture of the macaroni covered Christmas tree on page 94 gives an idea of how the macaroni covered wreath will look.

32. EVERGREEN WREATH

A. Materials: Students will need wire coat hangers, thin wire and evergreen boughs.

B. Procedure: Open the lower portion of the wire coat hanger to form a circle. Use thin wire to tie evergreen boughs to this ring, overlapping the boughs so the "stalk" of each bough is hidden. Tie a big red bow to the neck of the coat hanger hook if desired, and glass ornaments could be tied here and there among the boughs for additional decoration.

33. MACARONI TREE (Shown on page 94, lower left)

A. Materials: Tagboard, scissors, stapler, white glue, raw macaroni in a variety of shapes, and gold, bronze or silver paint are needed for this activity.

B. Procedure: Make a cone of tagboard. Staple the overlapped ends together. This will serve as a base for the tree. Paint a small area of the cone with white glue and fasten pieces of raw macaroni to this pasted area. Continue working on one small area at a time until the entire cone is covered with macaroni pieces.

When the glue has dried, paint the tree with gold, bronze or silver paint. A velvet bow or glass tree ornament makes a nice topping for the tree. The tree shown on page 94 is set on a footed goblet (from the dime store) which was painted to match the tree.

34. PAPER ANGEL (Shown on page 94, lower right)

A. Materials: Students will need tagboard, a styrofoam ball, stapler, glue and decorations as suggested below.

B. Procedure: The base for the angel pictured on page 94 is a cone made from tagboard. Wings were also cut from tagboard and glued in place. The head is a styrofoam ball, which could be decorated with cotton or yarn hair, and facial features cut from construction paper or felt glued or pinned in place.

The cone base and the wings were covered with scraps of a burgundy brocade fabric before they were stapled together. The trim is gold paper lace. Any pretty fabric and trimmings; such as rickrack, yarn, etc., could be used, or simply paint the cone and wings with tempera paint decorations.

Cone and Wing Patterns:

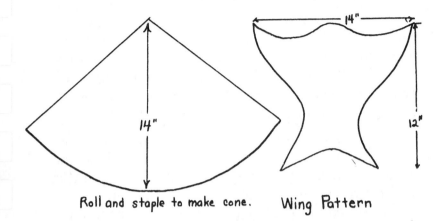

14"

Roll and staple to make cone.

14"

12"

Wing Pattern

LEFT: Partridge In A Pear Tree
RIGHT: Magazine Angel

35. PARTRIDGE IN A PEAR TREE
(Shown on page 99, left)

A. Materials: A tree branch shaped to resemble a tree, white paint (optional), a pot of wet sand or large pebbles in which to anchor the branch, white paper (adding machine tape, typing paper, construction paper, etc., work well), and gold glitter are needed for this activity.

B. Procedure: Anchor the branch in a pot of wet sand or large pebbles so it will stand securely upright. The branch may be painted white and sprinkled with glitter if desired.

Make paper partridges, following directions. Paste or tape partridges here and there on the tree branches. Pears may be represented by hanging gold glass ornaments on the tree, or actual pear shapes could be cut from gold foil and hung from the tree. Gold leaves could be cut and fastened here and there on the tree.

To make the partridges, follow these steps:

STEP 1: Cut four paper strips, each 1½" x 12", and stack the strips one on top of another. Roll about a 3½" length of the bottom strip to form the bird's head and staple this head loop to the other three top strips.

Example:

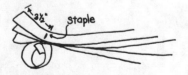

STEP 2: To form the body, leave the top strip straight and pull each succeeding strip about one inch shorter at the tail end than the one directly above it. Staple the strips about 2″ back from the head staple. Cut along dotted lines. Pull "crest" and "tail" strips between thumb and edge of scissors blade to form curls.

Example:

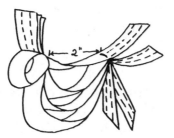

STEP 3: Place birds on tree branches. Add pears, as described, and leaves. Cover the pot holding the branch with gold foil or colored paper.

Example:

36. MAGAZINE ANGEL (Shown on page 99, right)

A. Materials: For each angel you will need one or two discarded copies of *The Reader's Digest* magazine, a styrofoam ball (or any other round object to serve as the angel's head — a plastic vitamin C bottle was used for the head of the angel shown on page 99), five 6″ round paper lace doilies, scissors, gold spray paint, glue and additional decorative materials as suggested below.

B. Procedure: Fold *every single page* in a copy of *The Reader's Digest* as shown in the example below. Sharply crease each fold line. Fan the pages out in a circle. This construction will stand erect and serves as the body of the angel. For a fuller angel, use two folded copies of the magazine stapled back to back. (The angel shown on page 99 was made from two magazines.) Spray the completed work with gold paint.

Example:

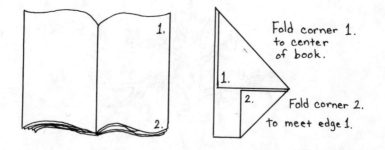

Fold corner 1. to center of book.

Fold corner 2. to meet edge 1.

Each arm is made from one half of a 6″ round lace doily, rolled to form a cone, and sprayed with gold paint. Glue the arms to the body.

Each wing is made from 2 paper lace doilies laid one directly on top of the other, for double strength, then folded in half and sprayed with gold paint. Put glue on the lower wing tips and tuck these glued ends between the magazine pages at the back of the figure.

37. ANGEL MOBILE

A. Materials: Wire coat hangers, wire cutters, small wooden beads or lumps of clay, pipestem cleaners, colored construction paper, paste, scissors and black thread are needed for this activity.

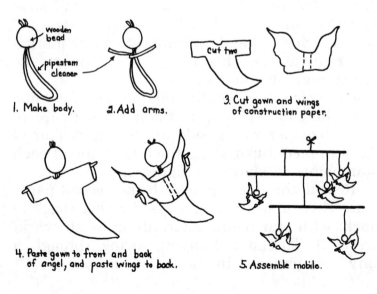

1. Make body.   2. Add arms.   3. Cut gown and wings of construction paper.

4. Paste gown to front and back of angel, and paste wings to back.   5. Assemble mobile.

B. Procedure: Cut lengths of coat hanger wire 6-8" long. Make angels as directed on preceding page. Hang the angels with black thread from the wires to create mobiles that move gently as the air stirs.

38. FOIL STARS

A. Materials: Students will need firm foil gift wrap or any other paper that will fold with crisp crease lines (construction paper does NOT work well, as folded lines are ragged), scissors, ruler and rubber cement.

B. Procedure: Cut two 5" squares of paper. (Squares can be larger or smaller if desired. Smaller squares are more difficult to fold.) Fold one square in half vertically, horizontally and diagonally. Open up the square and it will have fold lines as shown by dotted lines in figure 1. On each vertical and horizontal fold line mark a dot halfway (in this case 1¼") between the center and edge of the paper.

Cut each horizontal and vertical fold line from the outer edge up to the dot (see figure 2).

With paper wrong side up, fold each pair of sides to meet flush along the center line of each star point, as shown in figure 3.

Repeat this procedure with the second paper star. Then glue the two stars together, back to back, with star points alternating, as shown in figure 3. Thread a hanging string through a tiny hole punched in the tip of one point.

Example:

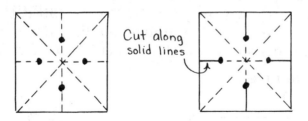

figure 1   figure 2

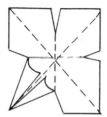   

figure 3   figure 4

39. REINDEER

A. Materials: Construction paper, scissors, a stapler, glue, tape and short sticks are needed for this activity. For sticks use popsicle, sucker sticks or straight sticks taken from dead tree branches.

B. Procedure: The head of the reindeer is made from a full 9 x 12″ sheet of construction paper. Overlap corners A and B in figure 1 and tape in place to form a pointed cone as shown in figure 2. The cone will be shorter in back than in front.

Cut antlers, eyes and nose from colored paper and glue them in place on the front side of the cone as shown in figure 3. A stick taped to the back of each antler and extending down onto the head section will hold it erect (see figure 4).

Example:

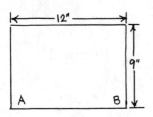

figure 1

figure 2

figure 3

figure 4

SECTION IV:

"VALENTINE'S DAY"

Heart-theme crafts galore that children can make to use as decorations, party favors, greeting cards or gifts for family and friends are described within this section.

TOP: Padded Hearts (3 examples)
CENTER LEFT: Arrow Party Favor
CENTER RIGHT: Valentine Marionette
BOTTOM LEFT: Dancing Heart Man

1. PADDED HEART (Shown on page 109, top)

A. Materials: Students will need red construction paper, scissors, facial tissues or old newspapers, a stapler and white glue. Decorations may be colored with crayons or felt pens, or could be cut from colored paper and pasted in place. Use rick-rack, lace, yarn, gold cord, etc., for border trim.

B. Procedure: Cut two identical heart shapes from red construction paper. Make them quite large — about 6″ across.

Decorate one heart with any desired design or message. Lay this heart, face up, on top of the other. Staple about 3/4 of the way around the margin to fasten the two hearts together. Put crumpled tissues or small crumpled newspaper pieces between the two hearts to give a padded appearance. Staple along the remaining portion of the margin.

A border trim of lace, yarn, etc., adds a nice finishing touch and also hides the staples. Lay a fine line of white glue around the edge of the heart, then press the trim into the glue. Let the work stand undisturbed until glue dries thoroughly.

2. ARROW PARTY FAVOR (Shown on page 109, left center)

A. Materials: Provide small, red and white striped stick candy, red and white construction paper, crayons, scissors and glue or a stapler.

B. Procedure: Cut two identical arrowhead shapes from construction paper. Decorate one with any desired Valentine design or message, using crayons or construction paper pieces glued in place. Staple the two pieces together along the front two edges as shown in figure 1.

Cut out two arrow feather pieces from construction paper. Decorate one, then staple the two pieces together along the top and bottom edges as shown in figure 2.

Slip the arrowhead over one end of the candy stick, and the feather piece over the other to make a Valentine arrow party favor. If pieces slip, spread white glue on the cellophane at each end of the stick candy. Press the arrowhead and feather pieces into the glue to anchor them firmly.

Example:

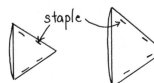

figure 1   figure 2   figure 3

3. VALENTINE MARIONETTE (Shown on page 109, lower right)

A. Materials: Red and white construction paper, scissors, string, glue and paper fasteners are needed for this activity.

B. Procedure: Cut red hearts of proportionate sizes to form the marionette's body, head, arms and legs. Cut small white hearts and glue them onto the head pieces for eyes, nose and mouth. Use paper fastener to join the hearts together. Punch a small hole in the top center of the marionette's head and tie a string through this hole. Wiggle the string to make the marionette move.

4. DANCING HEART MAN (Shown on page 109, lower left)

A. Materials: Red and white construction paper, scissors and paste are needed for this activity.

B. Procedure: Cut one large heart for the body and a smaller heart for the head. Paste the two hearts together as shown below. Cut

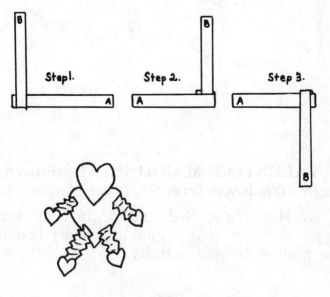

small white hearts for eyes, nose and mouth and glue them onto the head. The arms and legs are made from paper strips. Cut two strips and lay them as shown in step 1. Fold strip A over strip B. Then fold strip B over strip A. Repeat to form a pleated strip of the desired length. Paste the ends together. Make four of these pleated strips.

Paste the arms and legs to the dancing heart man. Hands and feet are made from small hearts pasted in place. Jiggle the Valentine to see the heart man dance.

5. HEARTS-IN-A-ROW

A. Materials: Provide red tissue paper and scissors.

B. Procedure: Cut a strip of red tissue paper 2 to 3 inches wide and 12 to 18 inches long (depending on size of hearts and length of row desired).

Fold the strip in half, in half again, and so on until you have a 2"- 3" square. Open up the tissue and use the crease lines to guide folding the strip into evenly-spaced accordian pleats (see figure 1).

With paper folded, cut a heart shape. Edges of the heart MUST touch the folded sides of the paper. These edges are NOT cut, which allows hearts from each layer of paper to be connected to each other along these fold lines (see figure 2).

Open up the paper to see the hearts-in-a-row, as shown in figure 3.

Example:

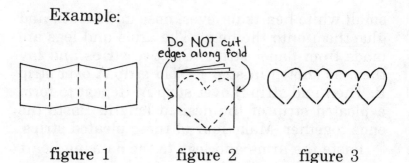

figure 1   figure 2   figure 3

6. HEARTS ON RIBBON

A. Materials: Students will need red construction paper, scissors, paste and ribbon. Crayons, felt pens, etc., can be used for decorations.

B. Procedure: Cut three hearts of graduated size from red construction paper. Write part of the Valentine message on each heart. Then

TOP: Paper Strip Hearts (2 examples)
CENTER RIGHT: Woven Heart
BOTTOM: Heart Beasts (3 examples)

thread the three hearts onto the ribbon. A spot of paste here and there between the ribbon and hearts will keep the hearts from slipping along the ribbon.

7. PAPER STRIP HEART (Shown on page 115, top)

A. Materials: Red, pink and/or white construction paper, scissors, ruler and a stapler are needed for this activity.

B. Procedure: From construction paper cut seven strips of paper, each about ½″ wide. Cut one strip 4″ long, two strips 6″ long, two strips 7½″ long and two strips 9″ long.

Example:

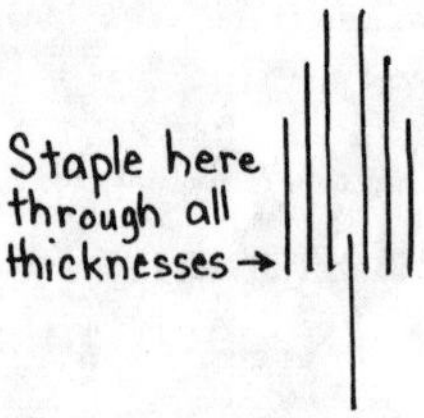

Staple here through all thicknesses →

figure 1

figure 2

figure 3

←staple here

figure 4

Stack the strips one on top of another, arranged as shown in the side-view perspective in figure 1. Staple through all thicknesses at the point indicated in the drawing.

Pull down the tip of the outer, 6″ strip on one side and align it with the bottom edge of the 4″ strip as shown in figure 2. Then in turn pull down the 7½″ and the 9″ strips, holding them in place as shown in figure 3.

Do the same for the 3 strips on the opposite side. Staple through all thicknesses to complete the heart shape as shown in figure 4. Tie on a hanging thread if desired.

8. WOVEN HEART (Shown on page 115, right center)

A. Materials: Provide red and white construction paper, pencil, ruler, scissors and paste.

B. Procedure: Cut a 4″ x 6″ rectangle of both red and white construction paper. Round off two corners and cut slits in each piece as shown below.

Example:

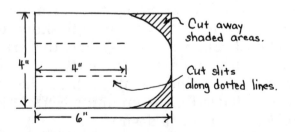

Cut away shaded areas.

Cut slits along dotted lines.

Lay the two pieces together to form a heart shape as shown in figure 1 below. Take strips from the red paper and begin weaving them in and out of the white paper strips as shown in figure 2. When weaving is completed, the finished work will look like figure 3. Paste the ends of the weaving strips to hold them firmly in place.

Example:

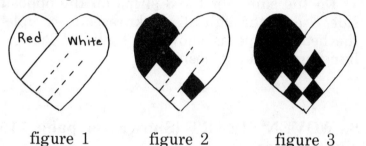

figure 1   figure 2   figure 3

9. HEART BEASTS (Shown on page 115, bottom)

A. Materials: Red, white and/or pink construction paper, scissors and glue are needed for this activity.

B. Procedure: Cut out paper hearts in a variety of sizes. Make many trial arrangements of the hearts to form the overall shape of an animal, bird, butterfly, etc. When the arrangement pleases you, paste the hearts onto a backing sheet. Very fine detail (such as the antennae for the butterfly shown on page 122) can be drawn with crayon if desired.

TOP: Heart Mobile (2 examples)
CENTER LEFT: Valentine Tree
CENTER RIGHT: Fabric Flowers
BOTTOM: Hearts-On-A-Stick

10. HEART MOBILE (Shown on page 119, top)

A. Materials: Students will need red construction paper, scissors, black thread and white glue.

B. Procedure: Cut a half-heart shape from red construction paper folded in half. Cut concentric half-hearts within this first one, each ¼″ to ½″ smaller than the preceding one (see figure 1).

Open up the paper and separate the concentric rings. Lay the largest heart on the table. Set aside the next largest heart - it will not be used in this mobile. Lay the third largest heart within the biggest. There will be a ¼″ to ½″ empty margin between the two rings. Continue setting aside every other ring and putting the next ring within the initial one, ending with the central, solid heart as shown in figure 2. (The rings left over from this construction can be used to make a second mobile.)

Spread a fine line of glue along the vertical **center fold line of all heart shapes (line A-B in** figure 2). Lay a firmly stretched thread into the glued line, leaving enough extra thread at the top for hanging.

Example:

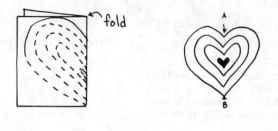

Let the glue dry thoroughly. Then hang the mobile where it can turn freely. Each of the concentric heart-rings will revolve independently from the others.

11. VALENTINE TREE (Shown on page 119, left center)

A. Materials: Provide a tree-shaped branch, a small container (use a tin can, paper cup, etc.), red, pink and/or white construction paper and black thread. Use pebbles, marbles or wet sand to anchor the branch. The tree branch can be left its natural color, or could be painted red, pink or white if desired. Additional, optional decorative materials are listed.

B. Procedure: If the tree branch is to be painted, do this step first and allow paint to dry thoroughly. Put the stem end of the branch into a tin can and fill the can with pebbles, marbles or damp sand to anchor the branch securely. Decorate the can as desired.

Cut heart shapes from colored construction paper. Hearts can be left plain, or could be decorated with crayons, felt pens, cut paper pieces, bits of paper or fabric lace, rick-rick, gold cord, etc.

Punch a small hole in the top center of each heart shape and tie on a hanging thread. Tie the hearts here and there on the branches of the tree.

12. FABRIC HEART BOUQUET (Shown on page 119 right center)

A. Materials: Students will need tagboard, straight sticks (sucker sticks, tiny wooden skewers, popsicle sticks, etc.), scissors, glue and red print fabric. For a vase, use a small tin can or paper cup filled with wet sand or pebbles to hold the flower stems in place.

B. Procedure: For each flower cut two identical tagboard hearts and two fabric hearts cut from the same pattern. Glue one fabric heart to the face of each tagboard heart. Glue the two hearts together, back to back, with the stick glued firmly between the two pieces as shown in the example below:

Example:

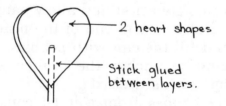

2 heart shapes

Stick glued between layers.

Make as many additional hearts as needed for the bouquet. Then anchor the stem end of each in the cup of wet sand or pebbles to form a heart-flower bouquet as shown on page 119. The cup can be covered with paper or foil and decorated if desired.

13. HEARTS-ON-A-STICK (Shown on page 119, bottom)

A. Materials: For each arrangement you will need 5 to 7 flat popsicle sticks, red, pink and/or white construction paper, scissors, cellophane tape, ruler and a paper cup filled with pebbles or wet sand in which to anchor the flower stems.

B. Procedure: Cut strips of colored construction paper, each strip about ⅜" wide (the width of the popsicle stick) by 6" long. Form loops with two strips and place one on each side of the popsicle stick, close to the top, as shown in figure 1. Fasten the loops to the stick by wrapping with tape as shown in figure 2. These two loops will form a heart shape at the top of the stick.

Fasten two more loops to form another heart shape lower on the stick as shown in figure 3. Continue fastening pairs of loops lower and lower on the stick to cover as much of the stick as desired.

Example:

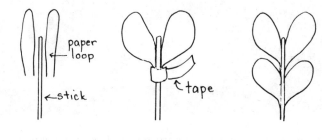

figure 1   figure 2   figure 3

TOP ROW: Valentine Lace, Photo Keepsakes (2 examples)
CENTER ROW: Cartoon Card, Burlap Valentine, Yarn Design
Valentine
BOTTOM ROW: Valentine Cut-Ups (3 examples)

Put the ends of 5 to 7 finished sticks into the paper cup filled with sand or pebbles (this anchors the sticks securely) to form a heart-flower bouquet as shown on page 119. The cup can be wrapped with paper or foil and decorated if desired.

14. VALENTINE LACE (Shown on page 124, upper left)

A. Materials: Thin paper (tissue, typing paper, etc.) and scissors are needed for this activity.

B. Procedure: Begin with a sheet of thin paper about 9″ x 12″ in size. Fold the paper in half, in half again, and in half a third time. This will produce a folded strip 9″ x 1½″ in size.

One side of this strip has folded edges only. Cut a series of variously-sized half-hearts from along this edge (see figure 1).

On the other side of the strip, there are two unfolded layers (the two side edges of the paper). Fold these two layers back out of the way and

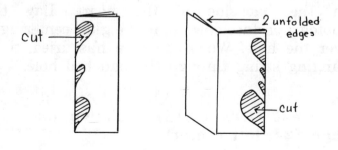

figure 1   figure 2

cut out half-heart shapes along the folded layers only (see figure 2). Open the paper to the repeated, lacey overall pattern of hearts.

15. PHOTO KEEPSAKE (Shown on page 124, upper right)

A. Materials: Provide self-hardening clay, a table knife, bright red acrylic or high-gloss enamel paint and brushes, colored yarn or string, rolling pin, white glue and small individual school photographs.

B. Procedure: Roll clay about ¼" thick. Use a table knife to cut a heart shape from the clay. Cut a rectangle hole in the center of the heart, making it just slightly smaller than the photograph being used. Punch a hole in the center top of the heart.

Allow the heart to dry thoroughly. Then paint the front surface and edges with bright red high gloss enamel, or acrylic paint thinned with a little water.

When the paint is thoroughly dry, spread a fine line of glue around the edge of the cut hole on the backside of the heart. Lay the photograph face down onto the glue, centering it over the hole. When the glue has dried, tie a hanging string through the punched hole.

16. CARTOON CARDS (Shown on page 124, left center)

A. Materials: Students will need colored comic strips pages from the newspaper, scissors, paste and construction paper. Students may use pen or pencils to write in the "balloons" to show dialogue for their characters.

B. Procedure: Cut favorite characters from the comic strips and paste them onto construction paper folded to make a greeting card form. Draw in "balloons" to show the conversation between characters. Write any desired message inside the card, using more comic cut-out characters or simply writing the message in traditional paragraph form.

17. BURLAP VALENTINE (Shown on page 124, center)

A. Materials: Construction paper, scissors, burlap, pens or pencils and paste are needed for this activity.

B. Procedure: Fold red or white construction paper to make a traditional greeting card form (see page 135). Cut a rectangle of burlap slightly smaller than the face of the card. Ravel the edges of the burlap to form a fringed border on all sides. Paste the burlap onto the card.

Cut heart shapes from red or white construction paper, decorate them as desired, and paste them onto the burlap background. Write a message inside the card.

18. YARN DESIGN VALENTINE (Shown on page 124, right center)

A. Materials: Provide construction paper, scissors, pencil, yarn scraps in red, pink and white, white glue and toothpicks.

B. Procedure: Cut and fold construction paper to make any desired card form (see page 135). On the card cover, lightly pencil in the desired design. The design should be simple with no fine detail.

Spread white glue around the margin of the design. Lay a strand of yarn into the glue, following the penciled outline. Spread glue inside this margin and lay yarn strands in rows, concentric rings, etc., to completely cover the paper in this area. Use a toothpick to press yarn rows firmly together, or to fit yarn into difficult contours. Work from the outlined border of the design towards the center.

Spread glue on one section of the background and lay in strands of yarn in a new color to fill this area. Continue in this way, filling the entire card with yarn. When the glue has dried, write any desired message inside the card.

19. VALENTINE CUT-UPS (Shown on page 124, bottom row)

A. Materials: Students will need old magazines, rubber cement, scissors and colored construction paper.

B. Procedure: Cut and fold construction paper to make any desired card form (see page 135). Cut pictures and words from magazine pages to create the Valentine message and illustration. Use rubber cement to fasten the pictures and words to the card.

20. FOOT LONGS

A. Materials: Adding machine tape and a pen or pencil are needed for this activity. Decorations can be drawn with crayon or felt tipped pens, or can be cut from colored paper or fabric and pasted in place.

B. Procedure: Begin at the free end of the tape and write any desired message, using as much length of tape as needed. Add desired decorations.

Roll the tape, beginning at the end of the message. The recipient unrolls the tape to read the card.

Example:

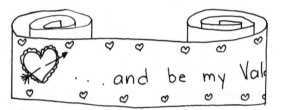

21. POP-UP HEART CARD

A. Materials: Students will need construction paper and scissors, plus any decorative materials desired, such as lace, ribbon, etc.

B. Procedure: Cut out the card shape as shown in the example. Fold along the solid line to make a raised ridge and along dotted lines to make valleys. Add any desired Valentine message, plus decorations. Fold the heart down inside the card as the card is folded shut. The heart will pop up as the card is opened.

Example:

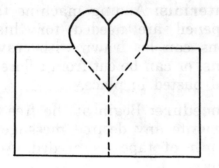

22. HAPPY DOG VALENTINE

A. Materials: Heavy construction paper or lightweight tagboard and scissors are needed for this activity. Features may be drawn with crayon or felt tipped pens.

B. Procedure: Cut separate parts from construction paper or tagboard and assemble as shown below. Add any desired decorative features.

Example:

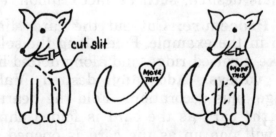

Dog will wag tail as heart tab is moved.

23. MOVING EYES VALENTINE

A. Materials: Students will need heavy construction paper or lightweight tagboard scissors. Features may be drawn with crayon or felt tipped pen.

B. Procedure: Cut separate parts from construction paper or tagboard and assemble as shown below. Add any desired decorative features.

Example:

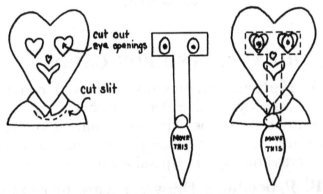

Heart man will roll eyes as tie tab is moved.

24. BROKEN HEART PUZZLE

A. Materials: Provide construction paper, scissors, and envelopes (See "How to Make Envelopes", page 135.) The card can be decorated with crayons, felt pens, or any other desired materials.

B. Procedure: Cut a heart shaped Valentine card and decorate it as desired. Then cut it apart like a jig-saw puzzle. Put the pieces into an envelope. The receiver must assemble the puzzle to read the message.

Example:

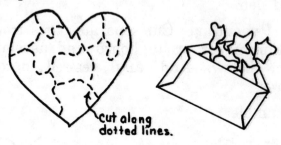

cut along
dotted lines.

25. TRIANGLE AND BOX CARDS

A. Materials: Students will need construction paper, pencil, ruler, scissors and paste. Decorations can be cut from colored paper or cloth and pasted in place, or they may be drawn with crayons or felt tipped pens.

B. Procedure: Draw a square or rectangle on construction paper. This will be the face of the greeting card. Decorate it any way desired.

To make a triangle card, draw a square or rectangle on each side of the first shape, making these the same size as the original shape. Add a tab as shown below. Fold along dotted lines,

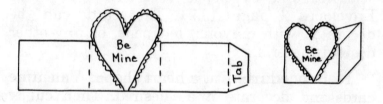

paste and tab, and you will have a three-dimensional, triangular stand-up greeting card.

To make a square card, draw three shapes of identical size in a line. Add a tab as shown below. Fold along dotted lines, paste the tab in place and you will have a square stand-up card.

Example:

26. QUICK SILK SCREENED VALENTINE

A. Materials: Provide construction paper, scissors, a plastic or metal embroidery hoop, 100% cotton organdy fabric, tempera paint, nail polish, firm cardboard and masking tape.

B. Procedure: These simplified materials and working methods make silk screening Valentine cards in quantities a quick and easy task.

Cut and fold construction paper to desired card size. Put organdy fabric into the embroidery hoop, stretching it as tightly as possible in the frame. Apply masking tape to mark off on the fabric the outside dimensions of the area to be printed (see figure 1).

Cut a square of firm cardboard and apply masking tape over one edge to make that edge as smooth as possible. The tape also keeps the card edge from disintegrating when wet with paint (see figure 2). This will be used as the squeegie.

Within the taped margins of the fabric, lightly sketch the desired design. Keep it simple, with no fine detail. Paint nail polish over all background areas, and any other areas of the design to remain uncolored in the finished print. Allow the nail polish to dry thoroughly.

Place the stretched fabric face down over the card to be printed. Pour tempera paint into the frame. Use the squeegie to spread paint evenly across the surface (see figure 3).

Example:

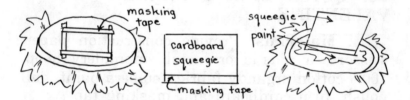

Lift off the frame carefully to avoid smears. Paint will have come through the fabric onto the card in all areas not blocked by nail polish. The texture of the organdy fabric will show in the print.

Set this card aside to dry and continue printing additional cards in this same way. When the tempera paint begins to dry and block holes in the weave, simply run it under a cool water tap to wash out the tempera paint build-up. Allow the fabric to dry, then continue printing.

27. TYPES OF FOLDS FOR CARDS

A. Materials: Red or white construction paper is needed to make these basic card folds.

B. Procedure: Fold paper as shown below to make various card styles.

Example:

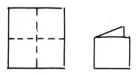

Standard Double Fold

Vertical Fold

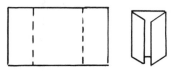

French Fold

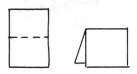

Horizontal Fold

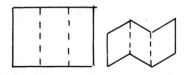

Accordian Fold

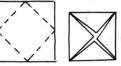

4-Flap Fold

28. HOW TO MAKE ENVELOPES

A. Materials: Provide paper, scissors, ruler, pencil and paste.

B. Procedure:

STEP 1: Lay the Valentine card on paper, and draw on the paper a square or rectangle slightly larger than the card.

STEP 2: Directly below this square or rectangle, draw another square exactly the same size.

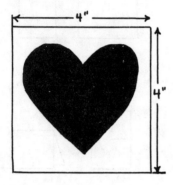

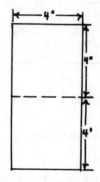

STEP 3: Add flaps, as shown below. Cut out the envelope.

STEP 4: Fold along dotted lines and paste flaps in place to complete the envelope.

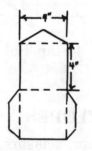

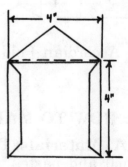

SECTION V:

"EASTER"

Ideas for baskets, bunnies and bonnets, plus a wide variety of egg decorating ideas to tide you through the Easter season are presented in this section.

TOP: Plastic Easter Basket, Bunny Basket
CENTER: Paper Plate Rabbit, Hatching Egg Card
BOTTOM: Spoon Bunnies (2 examples), Pop-Up Chick

1. PLASTIC EASTER BASKET
(Shown on page 139, upper left)

A. Materials: Provide a plastic berry box (used in produce markets for packaging berries, cherry tomatoes, mushrooms, etc.), scissors and weaving materials such as ribbon, yarn, string, cut paper strips, etc.

B. Procedure: Weave any of the materials listed above in and out of the open spaces in the berry basket to create a brightly decorated Easter basket. Fill the basket with artificial grass or crumpled tissue paper and use it to carry home decorated eggs, or use it as a pretty favor basket, etc.

2. BUNNY BASKET (Shown on page 139, upper right)

A. Materials: Students will need small paper bags, scissors and crayons, felt tipped pens or colored construction paper as desired for decorations.

Example:

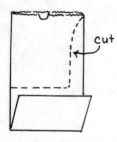

figure 1

figure 2

B. Procedure: With the paper bag folded shut, cut it as shown in figure 1. Use crayons, felt tipped pens or cut paper to create the bunny's face. Paper feet and a fluffy cotton tail may be added, if desired (see figure 2).

Fill the basket with artificial grass or crumpled tissue paper and use it to carry home decorated eggs, as a party favor basket, etc.

3. PAPER PLATE RABBIT (Shown on page 139, left center)

A. Materials: For each rabbit you will need two paper plates, pink tempera paint, brushes, scissors, colored construction paper and a stapler.

B. Procedure: Draw and cut out rabbit eyes, nose and mouth shapes from the center section of one paper plate. Paint the BACK (convex) surface of this cut-out plate and the FRONT (concave) surface of a second, whole plate with pink tempera paint. Allow the paint to dry thoroughly.

Cut two ear shapes from colored construction paper. Put the two paper plates with front (concave) sides together. Put the ear shapes in proper position between the rims of the two plates. Staple around the rims of the plates to fasten the plates together and to hold the ears firmly in place.

Use tempera paint or pieces cut from construction paper and glued in place to create any additional decorations desired, such as whiskers.

4. HATCHING EGG CARD (Shown on page 139, right center)

A. Materials: Students will need construction paper, scissors and crayons.

B. Procedure: Fold a 3″ x 8″ sheet of construction paper in half, crosswise. Draw an egg shape on the top layer. The top of the egg shape should run along the fold line (see figure 1). Cut out the egg shape, cutting through both thicknesses of paper. You will have two egg shapes, joined along the top fold line (see figure 2).

Cut the TOP LAYER only along a jagged, horizontal line. The top layer of paper will now look like the top half of a broken eggshell (see figure 3).

Close the top fold and trace its jagged outline onto the bottom, whole egg shape (see figure 4).

On the bottom, whole egg shape draw a chick's head peeping up over the jagged line (see figure 5). Decorate the egg with crayoned designs as desired.

When folded shut, only the whole egg is visible (see figure 6). When the top layer is lifted, the chicken-in-the-egg is revealed (see figure 7).

Example:

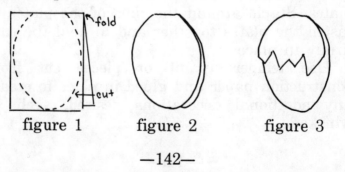

figure 1   figure 2   figure 3

figure 4

figure 5

figure 6

figure 7

5. SPOON BUNNY (Shown on page 139, lower left)

A. Materials: For each bunny you will need two flat, wooden ice cream spoons, white glue, scissors and colored construction paper. Decorations may be drawn with crayon, felt pens or tempera paint, or may be cut from colored paper or fabric and pasted in place.

B. Procedure: Lay the two wooden spoons with bowls one on top of the other and spread the handles apart to form the bunny's two ears. Use any desired materials to create the bunny's face on the bowl portion of the top spoon.

Cut an oval of tagboard to serve as the bunny's body. Glue the head to the body. Add any desired decorations, such as a fluffy cotton bunny tail, etc.

6. POP-UP CHICK (Shown on page 139, lower right)

A. Materials: Tagboard, scissors and paper fasteners are needed for this activity. Decorations may be drawn with crayon, painted with tempera paint, or cut from colored construction paper and pasted in place.

B. Procedure: Draw an eggs shape on tagboard and cut it out. Decorate the egg as desired. Cut the egg in half, horizontally, with a jagged line (see figure 1).

Draw a chick's head on tagboard. Cut it out and decorate it as desired. Paste the head to the backside of the lower half of the shell (see figure 2).

Overlap cut edges of the shell slightly. Fasten the two shell pieces together at one outer edge with a paper fastener. This serves as a hinge so the eggshell can be closed, then swung open to reveal the chick inside (see figure 3).

Example:

figure 1   figure 2   figure 3

7. BUNNY HAT

A. Materials: Each student will need a paper plate, two long, thin balloons and ribbon or string.

B. Procedure: Blow up the balloons and tie the ends. Staple the knotted end of each balloon to the top of the plate to serve as the bunny's ears. Ribbon or string, tied to each side of the plate, can be tied under the chin to hold the hat on the student's head.

Example:

8. PAPER PLATE BONNET

A. Materials: Provide paper plates, ribbon or yarn, scissors, staples and/or paste and cellophane tape and all sorts of scraps — feathers, lace, yarn, cotton batting, fabric, colored construction paper, netting, artificial flowers, etc.

B. Procedure: Using the paper plate as the base, fasten all sorts of scraps to the plate to make a beautiful, colorful, or downright zany Easter bonnet. Yarn, ribbon or string tied to each side of the plate can be tied under the chin to hold the bonnet on the student's head.

Students might enjoy a mock Easter Parade around the classroom to show off their creations.

9. SALT BOX RABBIT (Shown on page 147, left)

A. Materials: A salt box, oatmeal box or other round box, construction paper, scissors and paste are needed for this activity.

B. Procedure: Cover the box with colored paper. Then cut the fringed collar from construction paper.

Curl the fringe by pulling each strand gently but firmly between the thumb and a sharp object such as a scissors blade or ruler edge. Paste the fringed collar in place.

Cut ears, facial features and bow tie from construction paper and paste them in place.

10. EGG CARTON RABBIT (Shown on page 147, right)

A. Materials: A pressed paper egg carton, scissors, colored construction paper and paste are needed for this activity.

B. Procedure: Cut off and discard two end cups from the bottom section of an egg carton, leaving four rows of two cups each.

LEFT: Salt Box Rabbit
RIGHT: Egg Carton Rabbit

Ears, eyes, nose, mouth and whiskers can be cut from colored construction paper. Paste one ear to each of the top two egg carton cups and one eye to each of the next two cups. The nose, mouth and whiskers are pasted to the lower four cups.

11. POTTED PLANT

A. Materials: Provide a bare branch that resembles a tree or bush, blown eggshells, (see

"Blown Eggs" page 163), egg dye (see "How to Dye Eggs" page 164), pipestem cleaners, green tempera paint, green construction paper and scissors for this activity.

B. Procedure: Dip the eggs into dye to color them in soft, pastel hues. When the dye has dried, paint sepals with green tempera. Allow the tempera paint to dry thoroughly.

Push a pipestem cleaner into the needle hole in the sepal painted end of the eggshell. If the pipestem cleaner does not fit firmly in the hole, put a few drops of white glue on the pipestem cleaner, put it into the eggshell and allow the glue to dry thoroughly before proceeding.

Wrap the end of the pipestem cleaners around the branch, scattering the eggs here and there around the branch to look like flowers. A few leaves, cut from green construction paper and fastened in place on the branches with tape or glue, heighten the realism.

The branch may be anchored in a pot of wet sand or large pebbles for display.

Example:

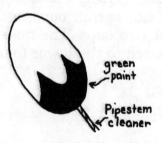

TOP ROW: Eggshell Garden, Eggshell Vases (2 examples)
CENTER ROW: Egg Candles, Sock Rabbit
BOTTOM ROW: Easter Lilies, Eggshell Mosaic

12. EGGSHELL GARDEN (Shown on page 149, upper left)

A. Materials: Students will need half eggshells, the bottom section of egg cartons, potting soil and flower seeds or plant cuttings.

B. Procedure: Put a half eggshell in each cup of the egg carton. Fill the shells almost full with potting soil. Use them as tiny pots in which to plant flower seeds or plant cuttings. The carton shown on page 149 holds dwarf zinnia plants newly sprouted from seeds. Since only. 2-3 seeds are needed per eggshell pot, one package of seeds will be enough for dozens and dozens of pots.

These tiny gardens make excellent, low-cost and highly welcomed holiday gifts.

13. EGGSHELL VASE (Shown on page 149, upper right)

A. Materials: Raw eggs, manicure scissors, regular scissors, colored construction paper, white glue, tape, fresh or artificial flowers and small plant cuttings or dwarf flower seeds are needed for this activity.

B. Procedure: Use manicure scissors to cut away the top of the eggshell and empty the contents. (Demonstrate this procedure, then ask students to prepare the shells at home so the raw eggs can be used, not wasted. They can carry the shells to school in an egg carton to protect against breakage.) The shells can be dyed (see page 164) or left their natural color if preferred.

Make a display stand in which to stand the egg (see page 163). Cut narrow strips of colored construction paper and glue or tape them onto the sides of the shell to form vase handles.

Put water in the shell, and add a spray of tiny, fresh spring flowers to complete the arrangement. Use artificial flowers if fresh flowers are not available, or put potting soil in the vase and add stem cuttings or seeds of dwarf, flowering plants.

14. EGG CANDLES (Shown on page 149, left center)

A. Materials: Provide eggshells, scissors, old crayons, paraffin or old candles, wicks or parcel post string, a coffee can, a flat pan of water, a hot plate and construction paper.

B. Procedure: First prepare the eggshell candle molds. Cut the tops from raw eggs (manicure scissors work well for this job) and empty their contents. The membrane lining should be left in each shell if possible. Students can prepare the shell at home so the raw eggs may be used, not wasted, then carry the shells to school in egg cartons to protect against breakage.

Place chunks of paraffin or old candles into a coffee can. Place the can in a pan of water and use low heat to melt the wax completely. Add bits of old crayons to color the wax as desired.

While this is heating, make paper collar egg stands as described on page 163. Place one egg, cut end up, in each collar.

Pour wax into each shell to fill it completely. When wax is slightly firm but still pliable, use a nail, knitting needle or similar tool to press a hole down through the center of the wax. Put a wick into the hole (use wicking from old candles being melted down, or use parcel post string dipped in wax). Pour a small amount around the wick to hold it in place.

As the wax cools and hardens, a depression will form around the wick. Pour in more melted wax to fill this depression.

When the wax has hardened completely and the shell feels cool to touch, gently tap the shell to break it and peel the shell from the candle. Place it back in its paper collar for display and use.

15. SOCK RABBIT (Shown on page 149, right center)

A. Materials: A sock, needle and thread, cloth scraps or old nylon stockings for stuffing, scissors, colored thread and embroidery floss or yarn for making facial features are needed for this activity.

B. Procedure: Cut and sew the sock as shown in the seven steps, stuffing each section of the doll as you proceed. Facial features may be sewn on with colored thread, yarn or embroidery floss. The tail is made from a yarn pom pom stitched to the body.

Example:

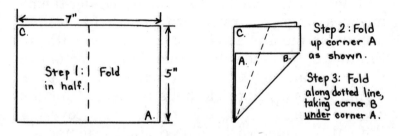

1.	Cut off toe of sock.
2.	Cut toe in two, and sew to make rabbit's arms.
3.	Cut foot as shown.
4.	Sew up legs, stuff and tie.
5.	
6.	Cut ribbing — Stuff & sew for ears.
7.	Sew on arms. Add face & tail.

16. EASTER LILIES (Shown on page 149, lower left)

A. Materials: Students will need white and green construction paper, scissors and paste. Paper for mounting the flowers is also needed.

B. Procedure: Cut and fold white construction paper as directed below to make each flower.

Example:

C.

← 7" →

Step 1: Fold in half.

5"

A.

Step 2: Fold up corner A as shown.

Step 3: Fold along dotted line, taking corner B under corner A.

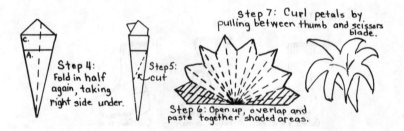

Step 7: Curl petals by pulling between thumb and scissors blade.

c.
A.
Step 4: Fold in half again, taking right side under.

Step 5: cut

Step 6: Open up, overlap and paste together shaded areas.

Cut lily stem and leaf shapes from green construction paper and paste them onto a mounting sheet. Paste flowers onto the stem as shown on page 149.

17. EGGSHELL MOSAICS (Shown on page 149, lower right)

A. Materials: Provide eggshells, egg dye (see page 164), white glue and paper. Students could save eggshells at home and bring them to school on the assigned day for this activity.

B. Procedure: Make egg dye in a variety of colors. A committee of students could dye a quantity of shells in each color and place them in different boxes according to color. Break the shells into relatively small fragments.

Use these shells to make Easter-theme mosaics. Lightly draw with pencil the desired design or picture. It should be simple, with no fine detail. Spread white glue on one section of the paper and lay shell fragments into the glue, using various colors of shells as needed for the desired design. Continue in this way covering the entire paper with colored shell fragments.

TOP ROW: Bleached Egg, Egg Loonies (2 examples)
CENTER ROW: Tie-Dyed Egg, Gold and Enamel Egg, Striped Egg
BOTTOM ROW: Yarn Wrapped Eggs (2 examples), Scene-In-An-Egg

18. BLEACHED EGGS (Shown on page 155, upper left)

A. Materials: Students will need hard-boiled or blown eggs (see page 163), egg dye (see page 164), old candles, matches, soft cloths and a container holding a mixture of 1 cup of cold water and 1 teaspoon of common household liquid bleach. For safety's sake, please read and follow all cautions on the bleach bottle label.

B. Procedure: Dye eggs as directed on page 164 and allow the eggs to dry thoroughly. Light a candle, tilt it and let wax run over the egg to create abstract patterns on some portions of the egg while others remain totally unwaxed. Let wax cool and harden on the egg.

Put the waxed egg into the bleach/water solution and allow it to stand for 2-4 minutes, or until all color bleaches off the unwaxed areas.

Let the egg dry, then use a soft cloth to rub off the wax. Color will remain bright in all areas covered with wax during the bleaching process.

19. EGG LOONIES (Shown on page 155, upper right)

A. Materials: Hard-boiled or blown eggs (see page 163), construction paper, cloth scraps, yarn, cotton batting, etc., as needed for decorations, scissors and white glue are needed for this activity. Eggs may be dyed (see page 164) or left in their natural color.

B. Procedure: Set the egg in an egg stand (see page 163). Cut colored paper, cloth scraps, yarn, etc., and glue these pieces onto the egg to create the desired realistic or silly animal or human face design.

20. TIE-DYED EGGS (Shown on page 155, left center)

A. Materials: Students will need egg dye in deep colors (see page 164), hard-boiled or blown eggs (see page 163), cotton fabric and rubber bands.

B. Procedure: Cut a piece of cotton fabric about 5″ x 6″ in size. Roll an egg in this cloth piece and fasten ends of the cloth tightly against the egg with rubber bands.

Example:

Put the cloth-wrapped egg into the dye just long enough to totally saturate the cloth. Remove the egg from the dye and let it dry, still wrapped in cloth, overnight. The next day, unwrap the egg to see the mottled, tie-dyed pattern of color.

21. GOLD AND ENAMELED EGGS (Shown on page 155, center)

A. Materials: Provide hard-boiled or blown eggs (see page 163), gold cord, white glue, high gloss enamel paints and brushes. A solvent for cleaning the brushes is also needed.

B. Procedure: Squeeze slender lines of white glue onto the egg to create whatever pattern is desired for the gold cord. Lay gold cord into the lines of glue, pressing down so the cord is firmly imbedded in the glue. Allow the glue to dry thoroughly.

Use enamel paints in several contrasting or harmonizing colors to paint areas of the egg's surface between the lines of gold cord. Be careful not to get paint on the cord itself.

Painting is easier if you set the egg in a paper collar (see page 163) during painting. Paint half of the egg, allow this area to dry thoroughly, then turn the egg in the collar to expose the other half of the egg.

22. STRIPED EGGS (Shown on page 155, right center)

A. Materials: Hard-boiled eggs or blown eggs (see page 163), egg dye (see page 164) and rubber bands are needed for this activity.

B. Procedure: Loop one or more rubber bands around the egg so the bands fit very snugly against the eggshell. Dip the egg into dye until the desired darkness of color is achieved. Allow the egg to dry thoroughly.

Remove the rubber bands. Areas of the egg covered by the bands will be white, making contrasting stripes against the dyed color of the remaining portions of the egg.

23. YARN WRAPPED EGGS (Shown on page 155 lower left)

A. Materials: Each student will need a hard-boiled or blown egg (see page 163), yarn scraps in a variety of colors, scissors, white glue and a toothpick.

B. Procedure: Spread white glue over one section of the egg. Lay rows of yarn into the glue to completely cover the egg's surface in that area. Yarn can be wound, coiled, zig-zagged, etc., to create any desired pattern. Use a toothpick to press rows of yarn closely together. Continue in this way, changing yarn colors as desired, until the entire egg is covered with yarn.

24. SCENE-IN-AN-EGG (Shown on page 155, lower right)

A. Materials: Provide raw eggs, manicure scissors, tweezers, white glue and decorative materials such as small artificial flowers, twigs, construction paper, beads, lace, small plastic animals, etc.

B. Procedure: Prepare blown eggshells as described on page 163. Use manicure scissors to carefully cut an oval or round "window" on one side of the egg.

The interior and/or exterior surfaces of the egg can be painted with tempera, water colors, or enamel paint if desired. When paint has dried, glue tiny decorative pieces inside the shell to create a scene to be viewed through the cut-out window.

Tiny twigs could represent trees, figures could be cut from colored construction paper, artificial or dried flowers could be used to create a floral display, etc. Put white glue on each piece and use tweezers to set pieces inside the shell.

Rick-rack, ribbon, lace, yarn, gold cord, etc., can be used to outline the cut window. This covers any ragged edges and also provides a nicely finished "frame" for the scene.

Make a display stand for the egg (see page 163).

25. CRAYON ETCHED EGGS

A. Materials: Each student will need a black crayon plus crayons of two additional colors, a hard-boiled or blown egg (see page 163), plus pins, nails, screwdriver blades or similar tools for etching designs.

B. Procedure: Eggs must be thoroughly dry and at room temperature. Solidly color the egg with one color of crayon. Then color a solid, second layer using a new color of crayon. Then apply a third layer, using black crayon.

Use a pin or other tool to scratch designs into the crayoned layers of color. Scratch through one, or two, or all three layers of color in various areas for color variations. Using tools with various types of points creates designs variations.

26. COMIC TRANSFER DESIGNS

A. Materials: Hard–boiled or blown eggs (see page 163), an old candle or other wax, scissors, tongue depressors or spoons, tape and colored funny papers are needed for this activity. Use recent issues of comic papers for the color will transfer better than if the ink is old and set. If desired, dye eggs in a very pale color (see page 164) before applying the transfer designs as directed below.

B. Procedure: Eggs should be at room temperature for best results. Cut out the desired character from colored comic pages. Small pictures are easier to fit on the egg's contours.

Rub the egg with a candle stub or piece of wax in the area where you wish the picture to be. Gently rub the waxed area with your finger tips to insure a smooth, even coating.

Lay the comic cut-out, colored side down, against the waxed portion of the egg. Tape the cut-out to the egg so it will not shift out of position while being rubbed.

Use a spoon or tongue depressor to rub firmly over all areas of the comic cut-out. This rubbing will transfer the colored ink from the paper onto the waxed surface of the egg. Remove the taped paper to see the transferred · picture.

27. BATIK DESIGNED EGGS

A. Materials: Hard-boiled or blown eggs (see page 163), crayons and egg dye (see page 164) are needed for this activity.

B. Procedure: The eggs must be at room temperature. If they are cold, the crayon wax will not adhere evenly. Use crayon (white or yellow are particularly effective) to color a design on the egg. Repeated patterns of stripes, squares, circles, etc., are especially pretty. Then put the egg in the dye and leave it for several minutes so the color will be very dark. The dye will color only the un-waxed background of the egg, making the pale-colored crayon design very pronounced.

28. EGG JEWELS

A. Materials: Provide hard-boiled or blown eggs (see page 163), glue and decorative materials such as sequins, paper lace, beads, tiny artificial flowers, etc.

B. Procedure: Place glue on the backs of decorations such as sequins, beads, ribbon, lace, etc., and glue them in place on the eggshell to create a jeweled appearance.

29. PREPARING EGGS FOR DECORATING

A. Hard-Boiled Eggs: Put raw eggs in a pan and cover them with cold water. Cover the pan and place it over medium heat just until the water comes to a full, rolling boil.

Leave the pan covered, remove it from the heat and allow it to stand for 20 minutes. The eggs will be cooked to perfection. Cool the eggs by placing them in cold water. Store hard-boiled eggs in the refrigerator.

B. Blown Eggs: Puncture a small needle hole through one end of a raw egg and puncture a larger hole in the opposite end.

Hold the egg over a dish and blow firmly through the small hole. The raw egg will come out the larger hole. (If it does **not** come out, enlarge the holes slightly and/or use a needle to puncture the egg yolk so it will fit through the hole more easily.)

Store blown eggs in egg cartons and handle them carefully to protect against breakage.

30. DISPLAY STANDS FOR DECORATED EGGS

A. Lifesaver Stand: Glue a candy Lifesaver to the end of an egg to be displayed vertically, or to the side of an egg to be displayed horizontally. When the glue has dried, the candy provides a stable display base.

B. Paper Collar Stand: Cut a strip of construction paper ¼″ to ½″ wide and about 5″

long. Roll it to form a circle and staple or tape the overlapped ends. Set the large end of the egg into the paper collar and the egg will stand erect and stable.

31. HOW TO DYE EGGS

A. Materials: Provide cups, vinegar, boiling water and liquid food coloring.

B. Procedure: For each desired color, mix 1 teaspoon of vinegar with ½ cup boiling water in a cup. Add 4-12 drops of liquid food coloring (depending on darkness of color desired).

Put an egg in the dye, turning it with a spoon so all sides are evenly colored. The longer the egg stays in the dye, the more deeply it will be colored.

SECTION VI:

"JEWISH HOLIDAYS"

A heritage rich in tradition provides inspiration for craft projects to be shared and enjoyed by children of all faiths.

TOP LEFT: Tu Bishvat Tree
TOP RIGHT: Simhat Torah Decoration
CENTER: Succah
BOTTOM LEFT: Dreidle - Type I
BOTTOM RIGHT: Dreidle - Type II

1. TU BISHVAT TREE (Shown on page 167, upper left)

A. Materials: Students will need cardboard tubes from paper towel rolls, heavy cardboard, scissors, white glue, green ribbon or construction paper and various colors of construction paper for decorations.

B. Procedure: Cut an 8″ disc from heavy cardboard. Set the end of the cardboard tube on the center of the disc and trace its shape. Cut from the center of this traced circle to its edges as shown in figure 1. Fold up the cut wedges. Apply glue to the underside, set the cardboard tube down into the cut circle and glue the wedges to the base of the tube as shown in figure 2.

Paint the tube and its base with green tempera paint. Allow the paint to dry thoroughly. Glue lengths of green ribbon or strips cut from green construction paper to the top inside of the tube and the bottom of the base as shown in figure 3. Cut flowers, leaves, fruit, etc., from colored construction paper and glue them to the strips to complete the Tu Bishvat Tree as shown in the photograph on page 167.

Example:

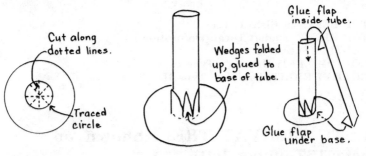

figure 1   figure 2   figure 3

2. SIMHAT TORAH DECORATION (Shown on page 167, upper right)

A. Materials: For each decoration you will need an apple, candle, apple corer, small paper plate (or a cardboard disc about 6″ in diameter) and greenery; such as evergreen twigs, sprigs of parsley, etc.

B. Procedure: Use an apple corer to cut a hole in the top center of the apple. The hole must be deep enough to hold the candle securely, but not go all the way through to the base of the apple (see figure 1).

Press the base of the candle firmly into the hole in the apple. If the apple tends to tip over, slice off the bottom to make a flat base.

Place the candle and its apple holder in the center of the paper plate or cardboard disc. Surround the apple with greenery as shown in figure 2.

Example:

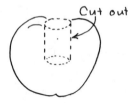

figure 1   figure 2

3. SUCCAH (Shown on page 167, center)

A. Materials: Provide tagboard, ruler, pencil, scissors and tape. Use cut paper decorations glued in place, or color the decorations directly onto the walls and roof of the succah using crayons, paint or felt pens.

B. Procedure: Use a ruler and pencil to draw the four 3″ square wall sections of the succah, plus the flap for joining, as shown in figure 1. (The succah can be made larger or smaller if desired.) Draw and cut out window and door openings as shown. Cut a 4″ square of tagboard to use as the roof, as shown in figure 2.

While pieces are still flat, decorate walls and the roof piece with designs of fruit, branches and/or leaves.

Score and fold along dotted lines and glue or tape the flap in place. Set the roof on the succah as shown in figure 3.

Example:

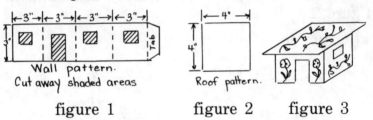

Wall pattern.
Cut away shaded areas

Roof pattern.

figure 1   figure 2   figure 3

4. DREIDLE (Spinning Top) - TYPE I (Shown on page 167, lower left)

A. Materials: Tagboard, crayons or felt pens, scissors, toothpicks and rubber cement or glue are needed for this activity.

B. Procedure: Cut a 2″ square of tagboard. Draw diagonal lines connecting opposite corners. In each section use crayons or pens to write one of the Hebrew letters nun, gimmel, hay and shin as shown. These letters are in-

—170—

itials for the Hebrew words "nitchs" (nothing), "gantz" (all), "halb" (half), and "shtell" (add). Other decorations may be added if desired.

Example:

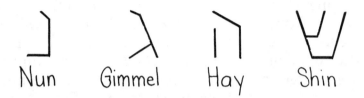

Nun   Gimmel   Hay   Shin

Push a toothpick through the center of the square. Put a little rubber cement or glue around the toothpick where it passed through the tagboard to anchor it firmly in place. When the glue had dried, the dreidle may be used for the traditional "put and take" games.

5. DREIDLE (Spinning Top) - TYPE II
(Shown on page 167, lower right)

A. Materials: Students will need tagboard, ruler, pencil, scissors, glue and lightweight paper such as typing paper. Decorations can be drawn with crayons or felt pens.

B. Procedure: Draw the dreidle pattern, as shown in figure 1, on lightweight tagboard. Cut it out, then decorate the squares of the driedle with the Hebrew letters nun, gimmel, hay and shin as shown in the preceding activity. Traditional designs of the menorah, candles, Star of David, etc., may be added.

Score and fold along all dotted lines. Apply glue to all tab sections (marked X in figure 1) and assemble to form the dreidle shape as shown in figure 2.

Cut a strip of lightweight paper 1″ x 9″. Apply glue to one side of the strip. Lay a pencil at one short end of the strip and roll up the paper firmly around the pencil, as shown in figure 3. Remove the pencil from the center of the roll. Apply glue to one edge of the roll and to the center top of the dreidle box. Let the glue dry until tacky, then press the roll firmly onto the box top to form the dreidle knob (see figure 4).

When all the glue has dried thoroughly, the dreidle is ready to use as a toy, a party favor, or as a container for a tiny Hanukkah gift.

Example:

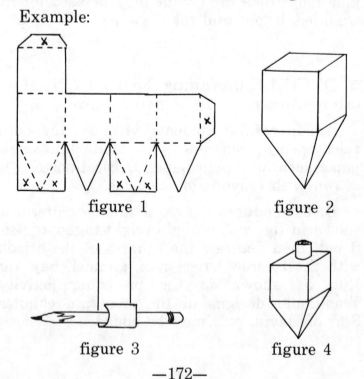

figure 1

figure 2

figure 3

figure 4

6. SODA STRAW STAR OF DAVID

A. Materials: For each star you will need 3 **paper** drinking straws, scissors, stapler and thread. Do not use plastic drinking straws, they cannot be flattened, so they are not suitable for this activity.

B. Procedure: Flatten all three straws. Cut one straw in half. Fold one whole straw to form a V-shape as shown in figure 1. Lay a half-straw across the open end of the V-shape and staple it in place as shown in figure 2.

Make a second triangle with the remaining straws in exactly the same way. Lay the two triangles on top of each other to form the Star of David shape as shown in figure 3. Staple the shapes together. Tie a hanging thread through the top star point.

Example:

 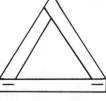 

figure 1   figure 2   figure 3

7. CHAD GADYA (AN ONLY KID) MOBILE

A. Materials: Construction paper, scissors, paste, plastic drinking straws and black thread are needed for this activity. Crayons or felt pens may be used for decorating the figure.

B. Procedure: Cut from construction paper figures from the traditional sedar song "Chad Gadya": the kid, cat, dog, stick, fire, water, ox, sholet, death angel and the Holy One (the Star of David is used to represent the Holy One). Decorate the figures with pieces cut from colored paper and pasted in place, or use crayons or felt pens for decorative details. Decorate both sides of each figure. Punch a hole through the center top of each figure and tie on a hanging thread.

Hang the kid and cat from each end of a whole drinking straw. Hang a second whole straw or a cut portion of straw from the first, whole straw. Tie the next figures to this second straw, moving figures along the straw to keep it balanced and hanging level. Continue adding straws and tied on figures, maintaining even balance. At the bottom of the mobile, hanging alone, is the Holy One.

Example:

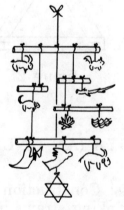

Tie a hanging thread to the center (or balancing point) of the top straw. Hang the mobile where it can turn in the breeze.

8. ISRAELI FLAG (Shown on page 176, upper left)

A. Materials: White and blue construction paper, ruler, pencil, scissors and glue or rubber cement are needed for this activity.

B. Procedure: Use a whole 8½" x 11" sheet of white construction paper for the background of the flag. Cut two strips of blue construction paper, each 1½" wide by 11" long. Cut two equilateral triangles, about 3½" long on each side, from blue construction paper. Cut away the center of each triangle, leaving a ¼" border, as shown in figure 1.

Glue the two triangles, one on top of the other, to form the Star of David as shown in figure 2. Glue the Star of David to the center of the white flag background. Glue one blue strip ¾" down from the top edge of the white flag background and the second blue strip ¾" up from the bottom margin as shown in figure 3.

Example:

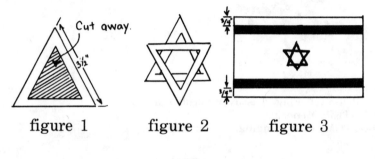

figure 1   figure 2   figure 3

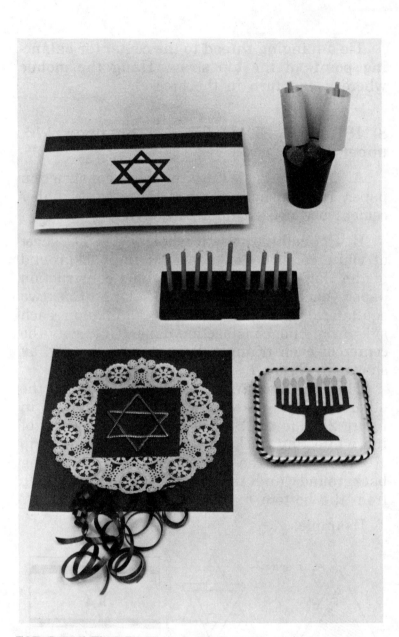

TOP: Israeli Flag, Passover Scroll Party Favor
CENTER: Menorah
BOTTOM: Wall Hanging, Purim Rattle

9. PASSOVER SCROLL PARTY FAVOR
(Shown on page 176, upper right)

A. Materials: For each scroll decoration you will need a small paper or styrofoam cup, scissors, blue tempera paint, brushes, white glue, yellow construction paper and 2 sticks (use skewers, pencils, lollypop sticks, or sticks cut from dead tree branches), each stick about 3½″ long. Candies, flowers, etc., are needed to fill the cup.

B. Procedure: Paint the cup blue. (Mix 2 parts tempera paint with 1 part white glue and paint will adhere to the slick surface of the cup.) Let the paint dry thoroughly.

Cut a 3″ x 12″ strip of yellow construction paper. Glue or tape a stick to each short edge of this strip and roll each stick towards the center to form a scroll as shown in figure 1. Write a child's name or holiday greeting on the scroll if desired.

Put flowers or candies into the cup and it is ready to use as a party favor.

Example:

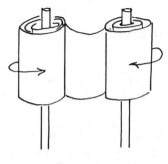

figure 1   figure 2

10. MENORAH (Shown on page 176, center)

A. Materials: For the base of the menorah use a flat board or a small, slender box. Also provide paint and brushes, thumbtacks, white glue and birthday cake candles. High gloss enamel paint was used for the menorah shown on page 176. Tempera paints could be used if preferred.

B. Procedure: Paint and decorate the board or box with traditional Hanukkah designs, such as candles, Star of David, menorah, etc. Allow the paint to dry thoroughly.

Apply glue to the heads of 9 thumbtacks. Glue the thumbtacks, head down, evenly spaced along the top of the board. Let the glue dry thoroughly. Press a candle down onto the point of each tack.

In the menorah shown on page 176, a small plastic ring box was glued to the center of the slender, flat box. This provides a raised platform for the central, lighting candle.

11. WALL HANGING (Shown on page 176, lower left)

A. Materials: Students will need blue construction paper, white lace doilies (either round or square in shape), yellow construction paper or gold paper medallions, gold braid, etc. for decorations, blue curling ribbon, scissors and glue.

B. Procedure: Mount the lace doily on blue construction paper. Cut a piece of blue construction paper to fit over the center section of the doily. Use yellow construction paper, gold foil, gold paper medallions, etc., to make a decoration in the center of the hanging. Cut several lengths of blue ribbon. Run them between thumb and scissors blade to curl the ribbon. Glue or staple these ribbons under the doily to finish the hanging as shown on page 176.

12. PURIM RATTLE (Shown on page 176, lower right)

A. Materials: For each rattle you will need 2 small styrofoam meat trays, 2 rubber bands, white glue, blue yarn, a yarn needle and dried seeds (corn, beans, etc.) or small pebbles, Decorations may be painted on the rattle or cut from colored paper and pasted in place.

B. Procedure: Put 4 or 5 dried seeds or pebbles in one meat tray. Spread glue along the top rim of this tray. Press the rim of the second tray down onto it to fasten the two trays together, as shown in figure 1. Put rubber bands around the trays to hold them firmly in place while the glue dries.

With yarn and yarn needle, stitch around the rim of the trays to form a decorative border as shown in figure 2.

Example:

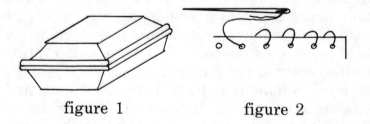

figure 1   figure 2

Decorations may be cut from colored paper and pasted in place as shown on page 176, or decorations can be painted if preferred. Mix two parts tempera paint with one part white glue. The glue makes the tempera adhere to the styrofoam surface and also gives a nice glossy finish to the dried paint.

SECTION VII:

"PATRIOTIC HOLIDAYS"

Presented in this section are creative projects that give children new ways to express love for their country and pride in its leaders.

TOP: Soldier's Hat
LEFT CENTER: Lincoln's Hat (above), Uncle Sam's Hat (below)
RIGHT CENTER: Paper Strip and Gummed Star Flag
BOTTOM: Tissue Fluff Flag, Hero's Medal (2 examples)

1. SOLDIER'S HAT (Shown on page 183, top)

A. Materials: One newspaper page is needed for this activity.

B. Procedure: Fold the newspaper sheet in half, crosswise. Fold corners A and B to meet at the center.

Next, fold up the bottom edges.

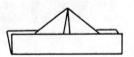

2. LINCOLN'S HAT (Shown on page 183, upper left center)

A. Materials: Students will need black construction paper, scissors, and paste or cellophane tape.

B. Procedure: Cut and assemble the hat following the steps given.

Step 1: Cut a piece of black construction paper 3″ x 5″. Roll to form a tube and glue or tape overlapped ends. This will be the crown of Lincoln's hat.

Example:

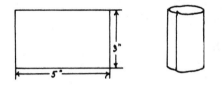

Step 2: Place the tube, open end down, on black construction paper. Trace its circumference onto the paper. Draw a larger circle around this traced circle. Cut out the large circle and cut away the small, center circle. This forms the hat's brim.

Example:

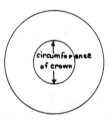

Step 3: Make slits about ½" deep at frequent intervals around the bottom edge of the hat crown. Fold out along cut lines. This makes tabs by which the crown and brim will be fastened together.

Example:

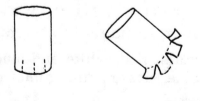

Step 4: Ease the hat brim down over the crown. Paste or tape the tabs on the crown to the underside of the brim.

Example:

3. UNCLE SAM'S HAT (Shown on page 183, lower left center)

A. Materials: Provide red, white and blue construction paper, scissors and paste or tape. Gummed stars are optional.

B. Procedure: Cut and assemble pieces for the hat just as directed for Lincoln's Hat, preceding activity, but use white construction paper for the crown and blue paper for the brim.

Cut narrow strips from red construction paper and paste them to the hat crown. Fasten gummed stars to the hat brim. (Stars cut from white paper can be used instead of gummed stars, if preferred.)

4. PAPER STRIP AND GUMMED STAR FLAG (Shown on page 183, right center)

A. Materials: Red, white and blue construction paper, glue, scissors and gummed stars are needed for this activity. A paper cutter makes fast work of cutting required paper pieces.

B. Procedure: Use a whole 9″ x 12″ sheet of white construction paper for the background of the flag. Cut a 4″ x 5″ rectangle of blue paper and glue it in the upper left hand corner of the white paper. This will be the field for the stars. Fasten gummed stars onto the blue field.

Cut 7 strips of red paper, each ¾″ wide by 12″ long. Glue one strip aligned with the top margin of the white paper, the second aligned with the bottom edge of the blue field, and a third aligned with the bottom edge of the white paper. In the open, white space between the top two strips, evenly space and glue in place two additional red stripes. In the open white space between the bottom two strips, evenly space and glue in place two additional red stripes. (This method assures even placement of stripes.) Trim away lengths of the top three red stripes that extend beyond the right hand margin of the white paper.

5. TISSUE FLUFF FLAG (Shown on page 183, lower left)

A. Materials: Provide white construction paper, red, white and blue tissue paper, pencils, rulers and white glue. Use a paper cutter to cut the tissue paper into 1-inch squares. Give each student a large quantity of these squares in all three colors.

B. Procedure: On white construction paper draw the design of the American flag. Spread white glue on one small section of the flag. Crumple the tissue squares into loose balls and completely cover the glued area with these tissue balls. Continue in this way, using appropriate colors in each section of the flag, until the entire sheet is covered with tissue.

6. HERO'S MEDAL (Shown on page 183, lower right)

A. Materials: Provide a compass, pencil, tagboard, colored construction paper, crayons, household aluminum foil, scissors, tape and straight pins.

B. Procedure: Use a compass to draw a circle on tagboard about the size of a half dollar. Cut out the circle. Cut a 2½" square of aluminum foil. Lay the foil over the tagboard disc and fold extra margins over and tape them to the back of the disc.

Use a pencil to press the desired message ("Hero", "1st Place", "Guest", etc.) onto the front surface of the foil covered disc.

Cut a 3" x 1½" strip of colored construction paper. Snip corners to taper one end as shown in figure 1. Decorate the strip with crayoned stripes or other design.

Staple or tape the medal to the ribbon. Use a straight pin to fasten it to the lucky recipient's shirt (see figure 2).

Example

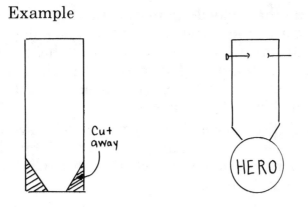

figure 1   figure 2

7. PAPER FIRECRACKER

A. Materials: Typing paper or brown wrapping paper, scissors and a ruler are needed for this activity.

B. Procedure: Cut a piece of paper about 8″ square. Fold up the bottom edge to within 1″ of the top edge of the paper (see figure 1). Fold the paper in half vertically (see figure 2).

Example:

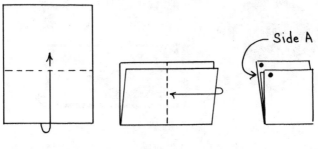

figure 1   figure 2   figure 3

Hold the folded paper with thumb and forefinger in the corner marked by black dots in figure 3. Raise the paper above your head and swing your hand and arm down quickly. The rush of air causes the paper to unfold with a loud pop like a firecracker.

If the firecracker does **not** pop when swung briskly, you are probably holding it by the wrong corner. Air must rush into the **unfolded** edges (side A in figure 3).

TOP CENTER: Benjamin Franklin's Hat
TOP RIGHT: George Washington's Cherry Tree
BOTTOM LEFT: George Washington's Hat
BOTTOM RIGHT: Fireworks Picture

8. BENJAMIN FRANKLIN'S HAT (Shown on page 190, upper left)

A. Materials: Students will need black and white construction paper, scissors and a stapler.

B. Procedure: Cut three pieces of black construction paper following the pattern shown in figure 1 below. Staple the three pieces together along curved edges as shown in figure 2.

Cut one piece of white construction paper following the pattern shown in figure 3 below. Cut along dotted lines. Pull cut strands between thumb and scissors blade to curl each strip. **Staple the uncut edges of this piece to the inside, lower edge of one black hat section. The hat now has a built-in, white, curly wig.**

Example:

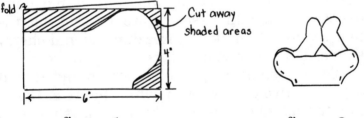

figure 1   figure 2

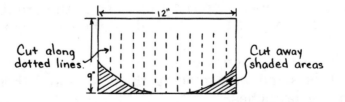

figure 3

9. GEORGE WASHINGTON'S CHERRY TREE (Shown on page 190, upper right)

A. Materials: For each cherry tree you will need a paper cup or small tin can, construction paper in red, white, blue, green and black, sand (or dirt, pebbles, etc., to anchor the branch), a small dead branch, scissors, stapler, tape and black thread.

B. Procedure: Cut a hatchet shape from black construction paper and glue or tape it to the front of the cup or can.

Set the branch into the cup and fill the cup with wet sand, dirt or pebbles to anchor the branch securely.

Use a penny or nickel to trace four circle shapes on red construction paper. Cut out the four circles and fold each in half. Open the fold, put one circle on top of another and staple along the center fold line (see figure 1). Fan out the four sections to make a three-dimensional cherry shape. Repeat with the other two circles.

Tape a short length of black thread (about 3″) to the two circles as shown in figure 2. Drape the thread over the tree branch as shown in figure 3.

Cut one or two leaf shapes from green construction paper. Tape or glue them to the branch over the loop of black thread as shown in figure 4.

Make additional cherry and leaf decorations in this same way, placing them here and there on the branches.

Example:

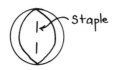
figure 1

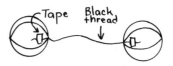
figure 2

figure 3   figure 4

10. GEORGE WASHINGTON'S HAT
(Shown on page 190, left center)

A. Materials: Provide black construction paper, ruler, scissors and a stapler.

B. Procedure: Cut three 5″ x 12″ strips of black construction paper. Cut each strip into the pattern shown in figure 1. Staple the three pieces together as shown in top view perspective in figure 2. If the hat is too large, staple edges a

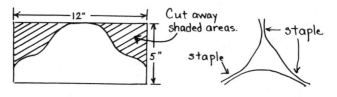

figure 1   figure 2

second time, farther in from the outer edges of each joint.

11. FIREWORKS PICTURE (Shown at bottom of page 190)

A. Materials: Provide drinking straws, construction paper and tempera paint in a variety of colors.

B. Procedure: Cut each drinking straw into 2 to 3 pieces to conserve materials. Each student will need a length of straw. For sanitary reasons, straws must not be shared.

Put a blob of tempera paint on paper. Hold one end of the straw almost into the paint and blow very briskly. The paint will spread in all directions, looking like the pattern of exploding fireworks in the sky. Blow again on any areas of the design where paint is still puddled. (If the paint does not spread into spidery-looking "legs" when blown, it is because the paint is to thick. Thin it with water and try it again.)

Continue in this way, using one or several colors of paint until the paper has a pleasing all-over fireworks design.

SECTION VIII:

"GIFTS"

Ideas for gifts that are quick, easy to make and suitable to give with pride for any holiday occasion are described within this section.

UPPER LEFT: Seed Mosaic Boxes (3 examples)
UPPER RIGHT: String Holder
LEFT CENTER: Napkin Rings (3 examples)
RIGHT CENTER: Orange Pomander Ball
BOTTOM: Seed Necklace (2 examples)

1. SEED MOSAIC BOXES (Shown on page 197, upper left)

A. Materials: Students will need small, sturdy cardboard boxes (jewelry boxes are perfect), high gloss enamel paint and brushes, white glue and dried seeds in a variety of sizes, shapes and colors. Dried beans, corn, apple seeds, fruit pits, split peas, etc., could be used.

B. Procedure: Paint the exterior of the box with high gloss enamel paint. Allow the paint to dry thoroughly.

Make many trial arrangements of the seeds on the box top. Try forming floral patterns, geometric designs, mosaic type pictures, etc. Use several types of seeds in the design for color and texture interest.

When the arrangement pleases you, lift one seed at a time, use a toothpick to spread glue on the seed, then set the seed back in place. Continue in this way gluing all seeds into place.

The completed box can be used as a container for a tiny gift, or can, itself, be the gift. The recipient can set it on his/her dresser or desk to store tiny objects such as pins, jewelry, paper clips, stamps, etc.

C. Variation: Instead of using seeds, decorate the painted boxes with gold cord, rick rack, paper foil medallions, pictures cut from old greeting cards, messages spelled with raw alphabet macaroni, etc.

2. STRING HOLDER (Shown on page 197, upper right)

A. Materials: For each string holder you will need a tin can with a plastic lid (a 1 pound nut can is perfect), white glue and string.

B. Procedure: Spread white glue around the top section of the can. Wrap string around the can to cover the glue completely. Tuck the beginning end of the string under the wrapping as you go.

Continue spreading glue and wrapping string until the entire can is covered. Tuck the end of the string under the previous rows of wrapping.

Use a large nail to punch a hole in the center of the plastic can lid. The recipient can put a ball of parcel post string in the container, threading the end of the string through the hole in the can lid. Pull on this end to dispense string as needed.

3. NAPKIN RINGS (Shown on page 197, left center)

A. Materials: Provide cardboard tubes from paper towel rolls, scissors, white glue and colored yarn, string, jute, etc. Spray shellac is optional.

B. Procedure: Cut rings about 1″ wide from the cardboard tube. Spread white glue on both the inside and outside of a ring, then wrap the ring with yarn, string, jute, etc. to cover it completely on both the inside and outside. Put a drop of white glue on the two string ends and tuck these ends under the wrapped strands to anchor them securely.

For ease in working, wrap a ball of string large enough to barely fit through the opening of the ring. Pass this ball in and out through the ring to wrap the ring. This length of string is usually enough to wrap the entire ring in one continuous strand, and the wound-up ball allows children to work without tangling the strand as they wrap.

The completed rings can be sprayed with clear shellac to give a durable, glossy finish if desired. DO NOT spray yarn - it becomes very bedraggled looking!

4. ORANGE POMANDER BALL (Shown on page 197, right center)

A. Materials: For each pomander ball you will need a firm orange, a quantity of whole cloves and ribbon.

B. Procedure: Push the stem ends of whole cloves into the orange. The cloves should be spaced so closely together that none of the orange is visible.

When the orange is totally covered, tie ribbon around it and add a hanging loop at the top. The pomander ball can be hung in a clothes closet or linen closet to keep the air fresh and scented with spice. The fruit will last indefinitely without spoiling, for the cloves draw out moisture. The pomander ball will lose its scent in time.

The high price of whole cloves makes this the most expensive project in this entire handbook. Do not attempt this project unless children are able to bring cloves from home. Or, try covering lemons, limes or tangerines in the same way as described for oranges. Because these fruits are smaller, fewer cloves will be needed for covering them.

5. SEED NECKLACE (Shown at the bottom of page 197)

A. Materials: Provide embroidery floss, embroidery needles, a large bowl of water and dried seeds of almost any kind. Use multicolored Indian corn, dried kidney beans, black-eyed peas, pink beans, garbanzos, small sized lima beans—simply choose those whose shape and/or colors you enjoy.

B. Procedure: Soak the dried seeds in water for 8-12 hours to soften them. To do this, put the seeds in a bowl and add enough water to cover them completely. Seeds will expand and absorb water, so you will need to add more water from time to time to keep them covered.

Cut a strand of embroidery floss about 12″ longer than the desired necklace length. Tie a knot about 6″ from one end and thread an embroidery needle on the other end.

Push the needle through one seed at a time, moving each seed tightly up against those previously strung. Use all one kind of seed for each necklace, or use a variety of seeds for shape and color variations.

Let the seeds dry completely. Then move seeds close together (they will shrink somewhat as they dry, leaving small spaces between seeds) and tie loose ends of floss together. Trim ends of floss close to the knot.

6. BREAD BASKET (Shown on page 203, upper left)

A. Materials: Students will need dough (recipe below), rolling pins, extra flour, a flat surface for rolling the dough, a sharp knife, an oven proof bowl to use as a mold, aluminum foil and an oven. Shellac is optional.

DOUGH RECIPE

3 cups flour
2 cups salt
2 tablespoons liquid vegetable oil
1¼ cups water

Mix all ingredients thoroughly, then knead with hands until dough is smooth and elastic. Store in plastic bags when not in use.

B. Procedure: On a lightly floured board, roll dough about ⅜" thick. Use a knife to cut strips about 1" wide.

Turn the bowl to be used as a mold upside down. Cover it with aluminum foil. This prevents the dough from sticking to the bowl. Lay strips of dough across the bowl, weaving them in and out of each other as shown in the basket pictured on page 203.

TOP ROW: Bread Basket, Snow-Scene-In-A-Jar, Storage Jar
BOTTOM ROW: Spool Racers (2 examples), Sewing Kit

Place the construction (with bowl still upside down) in the oven and bake at 350° for about 20 minutes or until the dough is hard and firm. Take it out of the oven and remove the woven dough basket from the bowl mold. Turn the woven basket right side up. Lay a strip of dough around the rim of the bowl, pressing down to securely fasten this strip to the woven bowl. This strip is strictly decorative. It hides rough edges and gives a nice finished appearance to the work. Decorate this strip with designs pressed in with finger tips, the end of an unsharpened pencil, the tip of a scissors blade, or any other device that gives a nice textured design.

Return the woven basket to the oven, right side up, and bake at 350° for an additional 15 minutes or so, until the entire basket is firm and hard.

Remove the basket from the oven and allow it to cool completely. The basket may be colored by brushing on water to which a few drops of liquid food coloring has been added - the color should be pale. Pale, golden bread color is especially effective.

When the color has dried completely, spray the finished work with clear shellac if desired. This gives a durable, glossy finish that can be wiped clean with a damp cloth.

7. SNOW-SCENE-IN-A-JAR (Shown on page 203, top center)

A. Materials: Clear glass jars with screw-on lids, tiny plastic figures of animals (from the dime store or brought from home), waterproof glue, tapioca, rice or white facial tissue and water are needed for this activity.

B. Procedure: Glue one or two plastic figures to the interior side of the jar lid. Let glue dry thoroughly.

Fill the jar with water and add ½ teaspoon of raw tapioca, raw rice or ½ teaspoon of facial tissues torn into teeny, tiny shreds. This amount seems small, but each of these materials will swell when thoroughly saturated with water.

Screw the lid onto the jar, then turn the jar over to rest on the lid. When the jar is shaken, the tapioca, rice or tissue shreds look like snow swirling around the animal. The "snow" gradually settles to the bottom of the scene.

This makes a nice gift for a sick classmate, or for a younger brother or sister.

8. STORAGE JAR (Shown on page 203, upper right)

A. Materials: Provide clean glass jars with screw-on metal lids, baker's clay (recipe below), shellac or plastic spray, plus an assortment of objects to press into the clay to produce textured designs.

BAKER'S CLAY

4 C. flour
2 C. salt   } mix together
2 C. water

Knead until dough is smooth and pliable. Add more flour or water if needed to obtain a good dough-like consistency. This makes enough clay for about a dozen lid decorations. The recipe may be doubled or tripled if desired.

The clay begins drying quickly. Store it in sealed plastic bags when not in use.

B. Procedure: Roll a ball of clay and flatten it with your hands to about ¼–½″ thickness. Mold it over a jar lid to cover the lid top and sides completely. Trim sides of dough even with the bottom rim of the lid.

Press objects such as pencil points, nail heads, screwdriver blades, etc., into the clay to form a repeated pattern of texture.

With your hands, sculpture additional decorative pieces of clay. Press the decorative pieces firmly onto the clay-covered lid.

Let the lids dry at room temperature, out of direct heat or sunlight, for 2—3 days. Total drying time will depend on the thickness of the clay. The lid can be baked in a 400° oven for about 30 minutes for quick drying.

When clay is thoroughly dry, spray with clear plastic or shellac for a shiny, durable finish. The lids could be painted with high gloss enamel if desired.

Screw the decorated lids onto the jars and they are ready to use as storage jars for pins, spices or what have you. Caution the recipient not to get the lids wet and not to store them in the refrigerator where moisture condensation may occur.

9. SPOOL RACERS (Shown on page 203, lower left)

A. Materials: For each race car you will need a wooden spool, a rubber band, a small nail or tack, a flat metal washer, a hammer and a short stick.

B. Procedure: A younger brother or sister, or sick classmate, will be entertained for hours with a pair of these spool racers. First drive a nail close to the hole in the top of the spool. Loop a rubber band around the nail, then push the rubber band through the hole in the spool. The rubber band should extend about 1/2-3/4" below the spool (see figure 1 below). If the rubber band is excessively long, double it.

Thread a washer on the rubber band extending below the spool. Put a stick through the rubber band loop below the washer (see figure 2). The stick should be off center—more extending on one side of the rubber band than the other.

Example:

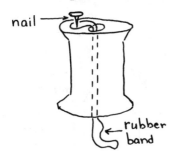

figure 1

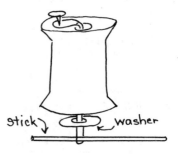

figure 2

Wind the stick until the rubber band is extremely tight. Set the spool on the floor and watch it race across the room.

The spools can be left natural, or decorated if desired. The spool racers shown on page 203 are painted with bright, high gloss enamel. Pin stripes and racing numerals are painted in contrasting colors.

10. SEWING KIT (Shown on page 203, lower right)

A. Materials: Small plastic pill bottles with lids, felt, scissors, needles, straight pins, thread, safety pins, etc., are needed for this activity.

B. Procedure: Cut a strip of felt about 4″ long and slightly smaller in width than the pill bottle is tall. It must be of a size that can be rolled up and fitted into the bottle.

Fasten needles, straight pins and safety pins into the felt. Wind thread of several colors in figure 8 patterns around several of the straight pins. Roll up the felt, put it into the pill bottle and put the lid on the bottle. This makes a compact emergency sewing kit.

Example:

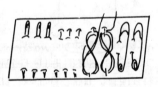
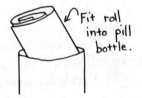

Fit roll into pill bottle.

11. SOAP BUBBLES

A. Materials: Students will need a glass or plastic jar with a screw-on lid, liquid soap, water, glycerin (optional, available at most pharmacies), plus bubble blowing devices as suggested.

B. Procedure: Here's a welcome gift for a classmate. But caution him to use the materials **outdoors.** Bubbles may leave stains on walls or furniture.

To each cup of water add 1 cup liquid soap and, optionally, 1 teaspoon glycerin. Glycerin is not necessary, but adds strength to the bubbles. Gently stir to mix — try not to create suds.

Pour the bubble mixture into a glass or plastic jar and screw on the lid. Along with the bubble mixture give one or more of the following bubble blowers:

1. A soda straw with one end cut at an angle as shown below. To use, dip the angled end in soap and blow through the straight end.

Example:

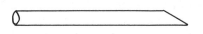

2. A wooden spool. To use, dip one end in soap and blow through the other.

3. A six-hole plastic holder for shipping 6-packs of soda pop. To use, pour bubble mixture into a flat pan. Dip the plastic straight down into the soap, then lift straight up. Wave the plastic briskly through the air to produce a multitude of huge bubbles.

4. A metal canning jar ring. To use, dip one open end in bubbles. Blow through the opposite end, or wave the ring briskly in the air.

5. A funnel. To use, dip the large open end in soap and blow through the small end.

6. A small paper cup with a hole punched in the bottom (use a pencil or nail to punch the hole). To use, dip the large, open end in soap and blow through the small, punched hole.

12. CLOTHESPIN WRESTLERS

A. Materials: For each set of wrestlers you will need two clip-type clothespins and a very sturdy rubber band. Decorations can be drawn with crayons, felt pens, tempera or enamel paint.

B. Procedure: Here's an entertaining toy to give a shut-in classmate, or to give as a holiday gift to a younger brother or sister.

Draw fierce faces and bright-colored wrestler's outfits on each of two clothespins. Loop the rubber band around one clothespin as shown in figure 1. Slip the second clothespin through the open loop of the rubber band as shown in figure 2.

Example:

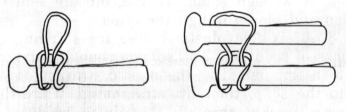

figure 1   figure 2

Wind up the clothespins until the rubber band is very, very tight. Set the wrestler's on the floor and watch them twist, turn and jump. When the rubber band unwinds, the wrestler's will stop. One (the winner) always ends up on top. It's fun to try to guess which wrestler will win!

13. STEM CUTTINGS (Shown on page 211, upper left)

A. Materials: Provide cuttings of such easily rooted plants as geraniums, philodendron,

TOP: Stem Cuttings (2 examples), Candlesticks (2 examples)
CENTER: Tiled Flower Pots (2 examples)
BOTTOM: Avocado Tree, Bulb Garden

wandering Jew, creeping Charlie, spider plants, coleus, dracaena, small-leafed ivies, etc. You will also need small glass jars. Decorative materials; such as aquarium gravel, marbles, pebbles, etc., are optional.

B. Procedure: Fill the glass jar full of decorative pebbles, marbles, aquarium gravel, layers of colored sand, etc. Add water to fill the jar. Put stem ends of cuttings into the jar, making sure ends are well under water. If necessary, push a pencil down into the decorative material, pull it to one side to create a hole, push the stem end down into the hole, then withdraw the pencil. (Or simply put cuttings into glass jars filled with water, using no decorative materials at all.)

Give these gifts with instructions to add water as needed to maintain the present water level, and to transplant the plant into potting soil once they have developed a healthy root structure.

14. CANDLESTICK (Shown on page 211, upper right)

A. Materials: Provide a collection of tin cans, bottles and jars of interesting shapes, and varied sizes, strong white glue, thumbtacks and decorative materials as suggested.

B. Procedure: Stack 2 - 4 containers on top of each other to create an interesting overall pattern for the candlestick. For safety's sake, make sure the stack is well balanced, with a wide container at the bottom for stability.

Unstack the containers and spread white glue around rims where containers join together. Press rims firmly together, reforming the desired stack and let it stand undisturbed until glue dries thoroughly (overnight is best).

The completed candlestick form can be decorated in many ways. In the photograph on page 211, the candlestick on the left (made from an inverted plastic flower pot and saucer) was simply painted a solid color with high gloss enamel paint. Additional decorations (stripes, floral or geometric patterns, etc.) could be painted on if desired. The candlestick on the left (made from a metal 6 oz. juice can atop a flat tuna fish can) was wrapped with white parcel post string. Try wrapping with several colors of string or yarn for a pleasing striped effect.

Put a generous blob of white glue on the flat side of a thumbtack. Set the tack, head down, on the center top of the candlestick. Allow glue to dry thoroughly. The recipient of this gift can push a candle down onto the upright tack point, thus anchoring the candle securely.

15. MOSAIC TILED FLOWER POTS
(Shown on page 211, left center)

A. Materials: Students will need small clay flower pots, white enamel paint (or whatever color matches the grout being used) and brushes, small mosaic tiles (those used on the pots shown on page 211 are ⅜″ square), grout, disposable containers for mixing grout and EITHER mastic or waterproof white glue.

In researching this project, every single tile dealer we contacted said he kept a box of odd lot or damaged sheets of tiles he routinely gave at no cost to teachers who come into the store and request them for school projects. The colors may not be the most choice, but you can't beat the price!

B. Procedure: Before clay pots can be tiled, the surface must be sealed. Otherwise the moisture from the white glue or mastic absorbs so quickly into the porous pot that tiles will not adhere well. To seal the pots, simply paint the area to be tiled (either the rim only, or the entire outer surface of the pot, whichever is desired) with enamel paint in color to match the grout being used. Allow this paint to dry thoroughly before proceeding.

IF MASTIC IS USED: Apply mastic to the surface of the pot in a thin, even layer, following package directions. Set tiles into the mastic in any desired pattern. Allow mastic to dry as directed on the package before applying grout.

IF WHITE GLUE IS USED: This adhesive is a little more difficult to work with, but is equally effective. Spread waterproof glue on both the pot and the backs of the tiles being used. Let the glue stand until it is thick and very tacky. Then set the tiles in place as desired. If you try to set the tiles with freshly spread glue, they will slip and slide out of position, which is frustrating.

When the mastic or glue is thoroughly dry, mix grout powder with water according to package directions. Use finger tips to spread grout across the tiles, making sure it gets down into and completely fills spaces between tiles.

After applying the grout, wipe off your hands and use clean finger tips to smooth the grout evenly. Then use a slightly dampened cloth to wipe smeared grout off the faces of the tiles.

When grout has thoroughly dried, a grout sealer may be applied according to package directions.

16. AVOCADO TREE (Shown on page 211, lower left)

A. Materials: For each tree you will need an avocado pit, three toothpicks and a small glass or jar of water.

B. Procedure: Push three toothpicks into the sides of the avocado pit. Set the pit in a glass jar, with toothpicks resting on the jar rim and the pit held up off the bottom of the jar. Add water until the bottom quarter of the pit is covered.

Give this gift with the following instructions:

1. Add water as needed to keep the bottom quarter of the pit covered.

2. BE PATIENT! It may take as long as 2 months for the sprout to appear.

3. When the tree is 6 – 8″ tall, pinch off the top 2/3 of this stem. This causes the plant to send out side stems, making a better looking, bushy tree.

4. At the same time the tree is pinched back, pot it in soil. The top half of the pit should be above the soil line.

5. The plant will eventually grow into a huge avocado tree (it takes MANY years!), but will not produce fruit.

17. SWEET POTATO VINE

A. Materials: For each vine you will need a sweet potato (select one with as many "eyes" as possible), 3 toothpicks and a small glass container.

B. Procedure: Push three toothpicks into the sides of the sweet potato. Set the potato, end first, into a small glass container. The toothpicks will rest against the rim of the glass, thus holding the sweet potato up off the bottom of the glass in the same way as the avocado pit shown on page 211. Add water until just the lower tip of the sweet potato is submerged. Tell the recipient of this gift to add water as needed to maintain this water level.

In about 2 weeks green sprouts will appear in the "eyes" of the sweet potato. These sprouts will soon develop into luxuriant, cascading vines.

18. BULB GARDEN (Shown on page 211, lower right)

A. Materials: A plastic margarine tub, small pebbles and 3—5 paper white narcissus bulbs or crocus bulbs are needed for this activity.

B. Procedure: Put a layer of pebbles in the plastic dish, then set the narcissus or crocus bulbs, FLAT SIDE DOWN, on the pebbles. Pour more pebbles around the bulbs to hold them securely in place. Do not cover the bulbs completely.

Add water until the water level touches the bottom of the bulbs. Tell the recipient of this gift to add water as needed to maintain this water level. He will have the pleasure of watching the bulbs sprout and grow, and in 3-4 weeks the plant will be in full bloom.

19. PAINTED FLOWER POTS

A. Materials: Provide clay flower pots, high gloss enamel paint, brushes and solvent for cleaning the brushes.

B. Procedure: Use enamel paint to paint any desired designs on the flower pot. You may wish to give the entire pot a solid color of paint for background, then add designs when this background color has dried, or use the clay color as the background and paint designs directly on the clay.

20. SILHOUETTES (Shown on page 218)

A. Materials: A dark room, a bright lamp, brown wrapping paper, a pencil, scissors, black construction paper, rubber cement and white mounting sheets are needed for this activity.

Silhouettes

B. Procedure: This is a time consuming project. In lower grades the teacher probably will need to trace, cut and mount all the silhouettes for the class. But no gift will ever be more treasured by a child's family, which makes the effort very worthwhile!

First tape brown wrapping paper to the wall in a dark room. Have a child sit in front of the paper and turn on a lamp so the shadow of his facial profile falls on the paper. Adjust the position of the child and light until you get a life-sized, undistorted shadow. Use pencil to trace the silhouette shadow onto the brown paper.

Carefully cut out the silhouettes from brown wrapping paper and trace its shape onto black construction paper. Cut out the black silhouette and mount it on white paper. Rubber cement is the best possible adhesive to use for mounting the silhouettes for it causes a minimum of warpage of the paper and smears can be rubbed off easily.

Back to basics & *the Spice Series*

MATHEMATICS

- ☐ **PLUS** — Primary Mathematics ● Grades K-4
- ☐ **Plus Volume I** ● Grades K-2 Duplicators from **PLUS**
- ☐ **Plus Volume II** ● Grades 2-4 Duplicators from **PLUS**
- ☐ **CHALLENGE** — Intermediate Mathematics ● Grades 4-8
- ☐ **Challenge Volume I** ● Grades 4-6 Duplicators from **CHALLENGE**
- ☐ **Challenge Volume II** ● Grades 6-8 Duplicators from **CHALLENGE**

METRIC SYSTEM

- ☐ **METER** — Converting to the Metric System ● Grades K-8
- ☐ **Meter Volume I** ● Grades K-3 Duplicators Introducing Metrics
- ☐ **Meter Volume II** ● Grades 3-6 Duplicators from **METER**
- ☐ **Meter Volume III** ● Grades 6-8 Duplicators from **METER**

SOCIAL STUDIES

- ☐ **SPARK** — Primary Social Studies ● Grades K-4
- ☐ **Spark Volume I** ● Grades K-2 Duplicators from **SPARK**
- ☐ **Spark Volume II** ● Grades 2-4 Duplicators from **SPARK**
- ☐ **FOCUS** — Intermediate Social Studies ● Grades 4-8
- ☐ **Focus Volume I** ● Grades 4-6 Duplicators from **FOCUS**
- ☐ **Focus Volume II** ● Grades 6-8 Duplicators from **FOCUS**
- ☐ **CHOICE** — Elementary Economics ● Grades K-8
- ☐ **CAREER** — Elementary Career Education ● Grades K-8
- ☐ **PRIDE** — Elementary Black Studies ● Grades K-8

SPECIALTY STUDIES

- ☐ **HOLIDAY** — Holiday Art Activities ● Grades K-8
- ☐ **CREATE** — Primary Art ● Grades K-4
- ☐ **CRAFT** — Intermediate Art ● Grades 4-8
- ☐ **NOTE** — Elementary Music ● Grades K-8
- ☐ **NOTE Volume I** ● Grades K-2 Duplicators from **NOTE**
- ☐ **NOTE Volume II** ● Grades 3-6 Duplicators from **NOTE**
- ☐ **GROWTH** — Elementary Health ● Grades K-8
- ☐ **PREVENT** — Elementary Safety ● Grades K-8
- ☐ **Prevent Volume I** ● Grades K-4 Duplicators from **PREVENT**
- ☐ **Prevent Volume II** ● Grades 4-8 Duplicators from **PREVENT**
- ☐ **STAGE** — Elementary Dramatics ● Grades K-8
- ☐ **ACTION** — Elementary Physical Education ● Grades K-8
- ☐ **DISPLAY** — Elementary Bulletin Board Ideas ● Grades K-8

PRESCHOOL AND KINDERGARTEN READINESS

- ☐ **LAUNCH** — Reading & Math Readiness ● Colors ● Muscle Builders
- ☐ **Launch Volume I** ● Duplicators from **LAUNCH**
- ☐ **Launch Volume II** ● Additional Duplicators from **LAUNCH**

MORE TITLES AVAILABLE ● SEE FOLLOWING PAGE

See your local School Supply Dealer
or mail to

The SPICE® Series
EDUCATIONAL SERVICE, INC.
P.O. Box 219, Stevensville, Michigan 49127

What is "The Spice Series"?

The "series", with each book having it's own title, was founded upon the theory that all teachers can use simple and explicit ideas to enrich any program. These ideas are produced in book form at a cost of $5.25 each. From the idea books, came the pre-printed duplicators ready for student use. The duplicator books are 40 pages and also $5.25 each.

LANGUAGE ARTS

□ **PRESS** — Elementary Newspaper Activities ● Grades K-8
□ **SPICE** — Primary Language Arts ● Grades K-4
□ **Spice Volume I** ● Grades K-2 Duplicators from **SPICE**
□ **Spice Volume II** ● Grades 2-4 Duplicators from **SPICE**
□ **ANCHOR** — Intermediate Language Arts ● Grades 4-8
□ **Anchor Volume I** ● Grades 4-6 Duplicators from **ANCHOR**
□ **Anchor Volume II** ● Grades 6-8 Duplicators from **ANCHOR**
□ **RESCUE** — Elementary Remedial Reading
□ **Rescue Volume I** ● Grades K-8 Duplicators from **RESCUE**
□ **FLAIR** — Elementary Creative Writing
□ **Flair Volume I** ● Grades K-8 Duplicators from **FLAIR**
□ **SCRIBE** — Elementary Handwriting

ORGANIZE A LIBRARY & DICTIONARY STUDY PROGRAM BY USING THE FOLLOWING DUPLICATORS

LIBRARY STUDY — LINGO & LOCATION ● CARDS & CATALOGS ● RESEARCH
□ **Library Studies Volume I** ● Grades 3-6
□ **Library Studies Volume II** ● Grades 7-9

DICTIONARY STUDY — WORD USE & ORDER ● SYLLABLES & SPELLING
□ **Dictionary Studies Volume I** ● Single letters Grades K-2
□ **Dictionary Studies Volume II** ● Letter combinations Grades K-2
□ **Dictionary Studies Volume III** ● Grades 3-6
□ **Dictionary Studies Volume IV** ● Grades 7-9

SCIENCE

□ **PROBE** — Primary Science ● Grades K-4
□ **Probe Volume I** ● Grades K-2 Duplicators from **PROBE**
□ **Probe Volume II** ● Grades 2-4 Duplicators from **PROBE**
□ **INQUIRE** — Intermediate Science ● Grades 4-8
□ **Inquire Volume I** ● Duplicators from **INQUIRE**
□ **ECO** — Elementary Ecology ● Grades K-8

MORE TITLES AVAILABLE ● PRECEDING PAGE

**Allow approximately 5% for shipping and handling.
(If payment accompanies order, Educational Service will pay all shipping and handling costs)**

Foreign customers contact our office for pricing.

School Name _____

School Address _____

City _____ State _____ Zip _____

Person Ordering _____

If you wish to have your order shipped to your home, please attach your home address on a separate card. Pricing subject to change without notice.

HOLIDAY

A Handbook for Teachers of Elementary Art

AUTHOR
MARY E. PLATTS
WITH PHOTOGRAPHS BY
GIL MASTERS
and
GORDON H. PLATTS

PUBLISHED BY
EDUCATIONAL SERVICE, INC.
P.O. Box 219
Stevensville, Michigan 49127